THE ORIGINS OF THE FIRST WORLD WAR

LUKE TRAINOR

HEINEMANN EDUCATIONAL BOOKS LTD
AUCKLAND LONDON

A HISTORY MONOGRAPH

General Editor: R.C.J. Stone

First Published 1973
Reprinted 1975, 1977, 1979

SBN 0 435 31900 0

ISBN 0 86863 507 3

The author and publishers wish to acknowledge with gratitude the editorial assistance of Professor R.C.J. Stone, History Department, University of Auckland. The author wishes also to thank Dr N.R. Bennet of the University of Canterbury for helpful advice on a number of points. Figures 1 and 4 first appeared in *The Press Weekly,* Christchurch, Fig. 3 in *Punch* 12 April 1905, and the remaining illustrations, including the cover, in the *Illustrated London News.* The maps were drawn by Mr J.K. Macdonald of the Geography Department, University of Canterbury. The cover photo shows the Kaiser and Count Moltke, the German Chief of General Staff 1906-14, on manoeuvres before the outbreak of war.

Published by Heinemann Educational Books Ltd,
P.O. Box 36064, Northcote, Auckland 9, New Zealand.
Set by City Typesetters Ltd, Parnell, Auckland.

CONTENTS

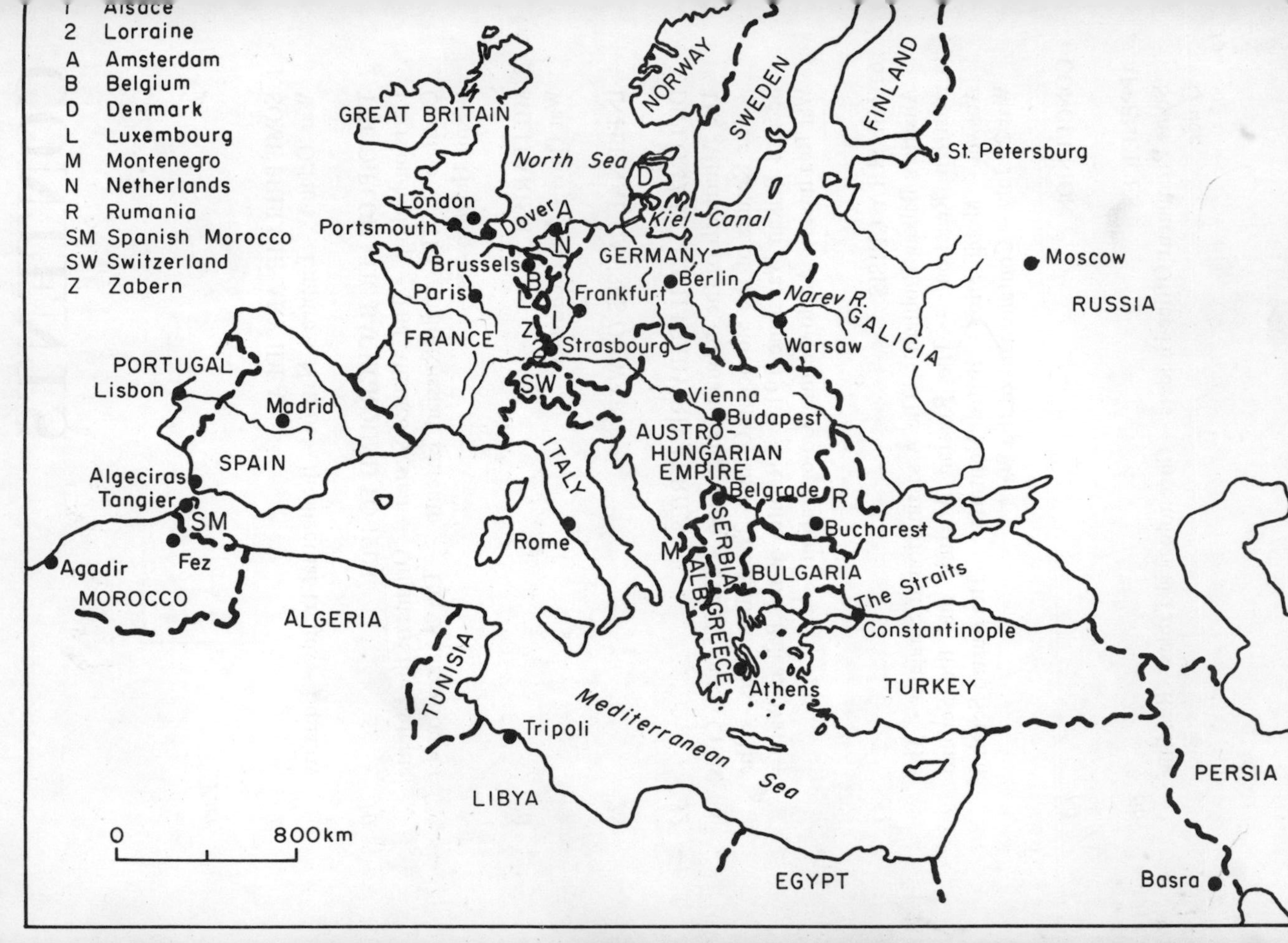

Europe in 1914

1. SOME PRELIMINARY IDEAS

WAR 'ORIGINS'

The question, 'What caused the Great War?' has been the source of continual debate. It was, of course, asked and answered during the 1914-18 war years, frequently for propaganda purposes. The Versailles Peace Treaty, however, by putting the war-guilt squarely on Germany, gave a great impetus to the controversy. Even now it can command space in popular German newspapers and magazines and, in Britain, the President of the Historical Association recently deplored the energy put into the study of the causes of the war rather than its consequences. Like most historical issues it has become more complex with the passing of years and the discovery of new evidence. A subtle change has occurred even in word usage, the tendency being now to write about war 'origins'. Presumably that is because the word 'cause' might be taken in the scientific sense of an event without which the consequence would not have occurred. Historians cannot make such assertions for they cannot construct a situation without the assassination at Sarajevo (for example) to see whether war would still have come about. A 'cause' to the historian is the set of circumstances that makes the event intelligible.

The story of the diplomatic crisis of the pre-war years is essential for an understanding of the causes of the war, as is also that of the arms race between the powers. Neither, however, makes sense by itself; there are certain preliminary ideas that help to make both the diplomatic interchanges and the arms race intelligible. If we examine the two pre-war crises which involved Morocco for example, we find that in the first, in 1905, the Anglo-French understanding was immeasurably strengthened and the foundation laid for the alliance which fought against Germany nine years later; and in the second, in 1911, the understanding was further strengthened and a sharp increase was given to European military expenditure. But why these Moroccan conflicts should have had such important European ramifications only becomes apparent if the idea of empire is studied. Similarly, the Balkan wars of 1912-13 seem to be simply the clash of armies by night, without an appreciation of the notions of race and nation as understood in eastern and central Europe at that time. In late nineteenth century and early twentieth century Europe, people were brought to the edge of war, and beyond, for ideas and for the material interests that buttressed them. If, as the U.N.E.S.C.O. Charter suggests, 'Wars start in the minds of men', it is there we must start a search for the causes of war.

EMPIRE

'Empire' is one of the ideas that dominated the last decades of Great Power peace. There were a cluster of images around the idea of Empire, but the central notion was one of domination. In the generation before 1914 in central and eastern Europe there were empires containing a multitude of ethnic groups usually with one dominant: the Ottoman Turks in Turkey, Prussians in Germany, Russians in Russia; and in Austria-Hungary the Austrians and Magyars dominated their respective parts of the so-called Dual Monarchy.

The British or French empires were, of course, geographically and constitutionally quite different structures, but there were similarities – the element of the predominant race, for example. The easy predominance of the British, or, as they called themselves in expansive moods, the Anglo-Saxons, was thought of as more than simply British imperial rhetoric. The difficulty of reconciling the ideas of nation and of empire was also common to all of these states. Minorities wished to express their own identity but this tended to weaken the empire they were part of. It is significant that some of those looking for a solution to Britain's Irish problem – or Ireland's British problem – looked to the Austro-Hungarian empire for precedents. In both empires, minority problems had reached the edge of violence in July 1914, but the Irish crisis was overshadowed because the Austro-Hungarian Empire got in first, attempting a solution to her internal South Slav problem by an invasion of the adjacent South Slav kingdom of Serbia and thus started the First World War.

Further, all the major empires tended to be expansive. A great variety of explanations have been advanced to account for that (see M.M. & M.R. Stenson, *Imperialism 1870-1914,* 1972), the most satisfying linking expansionism with contemporary European industrialisation and the growth of world trade. Important aspects of this connection were pointed out by J.A. Hobson, British economist and journalist, and V.I. Lenin, leader of the Bolshevik party in Russia, although the difficulty of formulating a theory that covered all types of empire remained. Both pointed to the basic demand for land that characterised empires, Lenin citing the German desire for Belgium and the French for Lorraine. The criteria for the extension of Empire included the resources and markets offered by the proposed acquisitions. The Russian government desired 'to preserve for ourselves the large Persian market for the free application of Russian capital and labour' (F. Kazemzadeh, *Russia and Britain in Persia 1864-1914,* 1968, p.461), and that caused continual disputes with the British and German governments. In Morocco, interest in the ore deposits in the Riff Mountains was heightened, in the case of some Frenchmen, by the loans they had extended to the Sultan. The object of securing a safe and profitable return on investment played its part, too, in the way in which domination was extended.

This use of capital as a political instrument was visible also in Europe. The access to loans on the Paris Stock Exchange was politically motivated and the Franco-Russian alliance was cemented with large loans. Over the period 1887-97, the French came to possess Russian government and industrial securities in excess of three million roubles. Russian loans of up to 500 million francs could be raised in Paris, under an agreement concluded shortly before the war, on condition that the funds were used for the construction of railways that would help to carry Russian troops quickly to the German border at the outbreak of war. Serbia, the landlocked kingdom on Austria-Hungary's southern frontier, provides a further example of the way in which domination could be informal, through trade or finance, rather than formal, through territorial annexation. Serbian trade was almost entirely across the border to the Dual Monarchy. When the trade treaty between the two countries expired in 1905, Austria-Hungary exerted pressure on Serbia to maintain it in a condition of dependence even to the extent of terminating imports from Serbia. The large part of Serbian exports being livestock, this was called the 'Pig War', but it could have been followed by an armed conflict, as was certainly feared in Belgrade at the time. It is perhaps characteristic of that age of competing empires that the Serbian capacity to resist and diversify her export markets was aided by French loans.

All the empires took great pains over the securing and protection of their major trade routes. The Suez canal and the Cape route have been used to explain British presence in Egypt and South Africa respectively. A German counterpart was the railway linking Berlin to Baghdad which contributed to the growth of the German trade with Turkey and helped reinforce the commanding position Germany acquired at Constantinople. It is important to distinguish between the way in which the railway was perceived by the British government and people and its actual importance. Turkey accounted only for about one percent of Germany's total foreign trade and although the trade with Turkey had grown fast, the other Great Powers had not been ousted.

Turkish Imports and Exports – Selected Countries ($ million)				
	Germany	Austria-Hungary	Britain	France
1900	16.1	22.1	54.5	28.9
1913	43.1	35.8	54.8	33.8

(Source M.L. Flaningam, 'German Eastward Expansion, Fact and Fiction', *Journal of Central European Affairs,* XIV, (4), p.322).

The rate of growth of the German trade did however cause particular concern in Britain, and the lucrative British sea-borne trade from the Persian gulf seemed destined to decline if the railway were extended beyond Baghdad to the gulf.

'Empire', then was one of the key words of the time; the domination of new areas through political or economic influence was one of its major characteristics. The aims of empire served the interests of the capitalist system: larger markets, cheaper raw materials, escape from the protective tariffs that impeded the previous highways of commerce, and outlets for capital. But Empire served a great many other interests as well. Soldiers and missionaries found their mission in it. It was sold to the people as providing employment, wealth, and prestige. It provided an emotional focus; some adopted it almost as a religion. Children were brought up to the glories of empire and the military values that were part of it.

Lenin saw the First World War as a war about empire. To him that was its distinguishing feature. It can be argued however, that imperial matters were quite secondary in the war. Anglo-French, Anglo-Russian and even to some extent Anglo-German, imperial differences were settled before the outbreak of war; Persia and Morocco were simply the *occasion* for European disputes. To say that, however, is to draw too sharp a distinction between the continental and the world empires, and to under-rate the importance of both. There was no escaping the reality of Britain's being an empire, as was made obvious by colonial contributions on the Western Front and at Gallipoli during the war. Professor Fritz Fischer, a well known German historian, has made clear too, the imperial nature of Germany's war aims. Also, we should not over-estimate the extent of the colonial settlement reached between Britain and Germany in 1914 – despite the good will of both Colonial Ministers, the agreement applied only to the future of the Portuguese colonies in Africa. In addition, Austria-Hungary showed some at least of the characteristics of the other empires. It regarded the Balkans very much as its sphere of influence and, while the war with Serbia was not one of annexation, it was fought to ensure unquestioned predominance for Austria-Hungary in the area.

NATION

'Nation' is a notoriously slippery word. In one sense it could be, and was, used as a reinforcement for notions of empire. The influential British organisation which fostered closer unity of the empire 1884-1893, the Imperial Federation League, contemplated substituting the word National for Imperial, the better to blur the distinction between the two. Enthusiasts for empire spent a great deal of time transmuting the idea of nation into that of empire in the popular mind. In both the British and French empires attempts were made to secure some form of common feeling based usually on racial lines.

Similar movements among Slavs and Germans, who were erroneously defined as 'races' at the time, were more obviously disruptive of the status quo because their absent brothers lived within the boundaries of other states. Thus pan-Slavism was a subversive force within the Austro-Hungarian empire and was a particularly acute problem because the dissentients had patrons outside the borders to support them. One of the reasons, for example, for the continued bad relations between Rumania and Austria-Hungary was the treatment of the Rumanian minority in the Transylvanian part of the empire. Of course, denial of self-determination or nationhood to minorities was of the essence of empire. The territorial idea of nation – that all within certain boundaries are subjects of one sovereign – was, throughout the second half of the nineteenth century, in conflict with the linguistic and cultural idea of nation. In a colonial empire, such as the British, there was the prospect of accommodating an assertion of local nationhood by a species of devolution, for example, the conferring of dominion status. In a more military empire such compromises seemed impossible – the very continuance of the empire seemed at stake. Austria-Hungary watched the almost complete dissolution of the Ottoman empire in Europe by the creation of the new nations in the Balkans. The next logical step was the dissolution of the Dual Monarchy to provide for the formation of a South Slav nation based on Serbia. The first world war escalated from a preventive strike by the Austro-Hungarian army at what it conceived to be a dire enemy to the continued existence of the empire. Although Austro-Hungary was the most severely affected by minority national problems almost all European states had them. Perhaps one in five of the European population before the war belonged to 'nations' struggling to secure territorial recognition.

Nation can be seen as a force dividing the European states and attacking their very bases – long established frontiers and traditional governments. At the same time it can be seen as a force making for unity. This paradox arises from the multitude of meanings that attached to the word and the variety of situations in which it applied. One example may help clarify this. In north-eastern France, Alsace and part of Lorraine had been ceded to Germany after the Franco-German war in 1871. The area had been

French since the mid-eighteenth century, in some parts earlier, and had been firmly French in sentiment since the French Revolution. The *Marseillaise* had been composed and first sung in Strasbourg. It was, to many Frenchmen, part of the French nation of which they were temporarily deprived and it became a focus for national sentiment, a centre-point for the 'National Revival' in the two or three years before the war. The French claim to Alsace-Lorraine was based on the idea of nation – long historical connection, kinship, and the desire of the inhabitants. The German claim to the area was also based on the idea of nation – a German dialect was spoken there and there were cultural ties and shared customs. Nation was, for many German writers, a living force that developed in peoples either consciously or unconsciously. Heinrich von Treitschke, a nineteenth-century German historian representative of this viewpoint, wrote:

> We Germans, who know Germany and France, know better what is good for the Alsatians, than those unfortunates who, due to their degeneration under the French, remain alien to the new Germany. We want to force them against their will to find themselves again.
> (M. Kitchen, *The German Officer Corps 1890-1914,* 1968, p.188)

The army was the instrument of this policy, and Alsace-Lorraine became the battlefield of two competing ideas of nation.

Nation, in all its various guises, held a high emotional charge in these years. Minority nations, without the command of local or national government, had to confine themselves to writings, sometimes veiled and allegorical, and secret meetings. Princip, who triggered the war by assassinating the Austrian Archduke at Sarajevo, was a member of one of the secret societies working in their different ways for the lifting of the Austrian yoke. Their ideas were nurtured in an atmosphere of mystery and ritual.

Majority nations, unifying their people with full public display, lend themselves to almost anthropological analysis. The young were inducted into the mysteries of the nation through their lessons and textbooks which emphasised the glories of the nation and empire. Away from school the influence also was strong. Baden-Powell saw his Boy Scouts, who were to have been called Imperial Scouts, as a preparation for war and the defence of the British Empire. Army officers were the priests of the new religion and its rituals included eleborate marches and pageants. It had festivals specially formed. Lord Meath, who introduced Empire Day into Britain in 1904, claimed that it was partly responsible for the influx of volunteers in 1914. J.A. Hobson, claimed that the whole ritual, with the saluting of the flag, was 'a semi-conscious endeavour to direct to patriotic purposes the fund of superstition liberated by the weakening of religious attachments.' (J.O. Springhall 'Lord Meath, Youth and Empire', *Journal of Contemporary History,* V (4), 1970, p.107.) Ample symbols were provided. In Paris the statue representing Strasbourg was veiled in mourning from 1871 until Alsace-Lorraine was regained in 1918. The arts, too, were called into service. Sometimes, as with Elgar providing pomp and circumstance, they brought quality, but sometimes only quantity: 50,000 poems a day were received by German newspapers early in the war. In England the *Daily Graphic* found 'touching' the poem of a twelve year old girl:

Down with the Germans, down with them all;
O Army and Navy, be sure of their fall.
Spare not one of them, those deceitful spies;
Cut their tongues, pull out their eyes.
Down with them all!

Much pre-war national cant had strongly aggressive and military undertones, so it is not surprising to find writers greeting the war with relief. Julian Grenfell, an English poet, commented 'I *adore* war, it is like a big picnic!' This military element, so frequently linked with ideas of nation and empire, is considered more fully in Chapter 3. It would be a perversion to suggest that aggressive nationalism had conquered Europe by 1914; there is ample evidence of the peaceful disposition of so many of the inhabitants of all the countries. Still, the extent of its spread is striking. Perhaps it would not be unreasonable to suggest a connection between nationalism and the surprisingly high level of voluntary enlistments which brought the British and Imperial forces to 4¼ million by November 1916.

INTELLECTUAL TRENDS

The sentiments of nation and empire, with their frequent aggressive and military connections, derived some of their support from the general movement of ideas in these years. This is difficult to demonstrate, just as it is difficult to make the link between the moon and the ripples that lap our feet at the water's edge. Two points might be suggested. First, the men in positions of influence in 1914 were of the generation heavily influenced by debased Darwinism. Evolution was taken from its own field and applied to society, providing certain natural laws which would ensure progress if obeyed. Man survived, and proved his moral worthiness to survive, by a struggle for existence, just as natural selection proceeded by a struggle among the species. This creed had the advantage of being easily understood and marvellously adaptable. It could be, and was, applied to international racial and social conflict. Moltke and Conrad, the Chiefs of Staff for the Central Powers, wrote frequently in these terms and many other statesmen and leaders, in all the major nations, accepted the necessity, even the desirability, of struggle among the nations.

Second, a younger group of thinkers from the 1890 s on reacted against this Darwinian pseudo-science. In probing deeper into men's motives they tended to put an emphasis on the importance of instinct and intuition. In Bergson, Weber, Durkheim, Sorel and other thinkers on the continent, there is a marked preoccupation with the role of the unconscious. There was a belief that some knowledge of human affairs came, not from supposed laws, but from flashes of intuition or the creation of convenient fictions or myths. Much of this foreshadows Freud, but his ideas cannot be said to have been widely influential until after the war. This theme in modern thought did not displace reason as the guide, but it did modify it. In the way in which the ideas of these men filtered down into society, concern for reason as the measure of things was weakened. Bergson laid emphasis on the vital impulse in man, an idea close to animal instinct, Sorel praised the value of violence and was strongly anti-parliamentary. Indeed, the fundamentals of parliamentary democracy were criticised by political theorists. Much of this criticism was justified, but it might be argued that the undervaluing of rational discussion for the resolution of conflict heightened the tensions in pre-war society. The political meaning of the development was noted by Sir Ernest Barker, the British political theorist, at the outbreak of war: 'Conservatism with its appeal to sentiment and its antipathy to doctrinaire Radicalism, is the residuary legatee of all anti-intellectual movements' (*Political Thought in England,* 1915, p.248.)

EQUALITY

In Britain, France, Germany and Russia notions of empire and nation found their readiest support at the Right end of the political spectrum. There was a high correlation between militant concepts of empire and nation and conservative views in domestic matters. The conflict between these views and those held by Radical and Socialist groups are examined below for their contribution to the outbreak of war. It will be sufficient here to point out the challenge of Socialist ideas to the existing order. The variety of views among the 4¼ million Socialists in the world in 1914 can, for convenience, be brought under the umbrella of the term 'Equality'. They sought a reduction of the inequalities in education, living standard and political participation to allow men and women equal opportunity of fully human development. The existing system of capitalism prevented that and would have to be altered or abolished. Empire arose from capitalism and would have no part in the new order. There was not agreement over whether or not it inevitably led to war. The Socialists' organisation, the International, was to have settled the question at a meeting in Vienna scheduled for August 1914 but the advent of war prevented that. Socialists also threatened the idea of nation, especially when it was associated with aggression and the suppression of minorities. The French worker, they claimed, had more in common with his German counterpart than with his French capitalist employer. The movement, however, was not successful in completely conquering national feelings. A prominent German Socialist wrote to a French colleague, 'What the Prussian boot means to you, the Russian knout means to us.' Perhaps the sharpest point of conflict with the state in the pre-war years was over military preparations for war.

This was more than simply the reaction of men who saw strikes suppressed by the army with bloodshed. War was for capitalist interests, but its chief victims would be the workers. Although there were differences of view over the efficacy of declaring a General Strike in which all workers would participate, still the threat of such action was used as a deterrent to war. The chief French union, the C.G.T., issued such a threat in 1912 at the time of the Balkan war. In Italy a strike against military service in Tripoli was led by a young Socialist called Benito Mussolini. Despite the weaknesses and divisions, the Socialist world-view challenged the existing order at all points and showed every sign of growing rather than weakening.

However, in July 1914, the International was as slow to recognise the coming crisis as the diplomats. When it did, it was unsuccessful in concerting action. In Germany, the Chancellor was careful to ensure that war was presented as having been provoked by Russia. The Social Democrat leaders were won by the possible benefits of co-operation with the government, the dangers of opposition (the army was awaiting an excuse to arrest them) and the fear of Rosa Luxemburg and other critics within the party taking control. The party leadership had long ceased to be revolutionary and could be bought off by concessions as with bourgeois parties. In France, whatever slim chance there was of working class resistance to the war was ended by the assassination of Jaurés, the Socialist leader, in the midst of a campaign to rouse the people against militarism. His death on 31 July was perhaps symbolic of the victory of violence.

2. THE DIPLOMATIC BACKGROUND TO 1908

DECISION-MAKING

One may write, 'Britain decided to take a strong line against German demands for a considerable French concession over Morocco in 1911,' while recognising that behind the decision there lies a multitude of discussions, notes, memoranda and pressures. This process of decision-making has an importance of its own. The bald statement that Britain decided to take a strong line conceals the fact that it was announced by Lloyd George, the Chancellor of the Exchequer, rather than by the Foreign Secretary, Grey. That was a point of importance, for Lloyd George was trusted by the Radical group within the British Liberal government, while they distrusted Grey and his policy of *Entente*, which they took to mean supporting extravagant French pretensions instead of looking for an understanding with the German government. The minutes written on incoming despatches and the personal correspondence of the permanent staff of the Foreign Office also modify our view. In July 1911 the German government had the gunboat *Panther* at the south Moroccan port of Agadir. When it became obvious that the German government was demanding the greater part of the French Congo as the price of their allowing the French a free hand in Morocco, Sir Eyre Crowe, a prominent Foreign Office expert on Germany, wrote: 'This is a trial of strength if anything. Concession means not loss of interests or loss of prestige. It means defeat with all its inevitable consequences.' On this occasion, as on so many others in the pre-war years, the British officials took a strong anti-German attitude and determined to hold tight to the Entente with France and Russia. Although their influence varied, it is obviously important to understand this general tendency in their advice. On this occasion the ministers were not only the nominal decision-makers, as they must be in accord with the practice of Cabinet responsibility, but the practical ones as well. The ministers in charge of naval affairs and of finance were particularly active. 'In fact, I believe', wrote the permanent head of the Foreign Office, 'they were a little disappointed that war with

Germany did not occur. Winston [Churchill, First Lord of the Admiralty] came to see me every morning and Lloyd George [Chancellor of the Exchequer] came once, and I was struck by the determination of both of them, not to permit Germany to assume the role of bully and at their belief that the present moment was an exceedingly favourable one to open hostilities.' The study could go further to include the influence of parliament, business interests, newspapers and so on. It is worthwhile recognising this network of interests behind decisions although, of course, it is not always fruitful to study decisions at such depth. International relations is not a self-contained system like a game of chess played by two computers, but more resembles a hand of contract bridge with each player, bound by obligations to a partner, but making decisions in view of his own outlook and the influences on him.

THE ALLIANCE SYSTEM

The obligations that bound the European powers before the war had their origins chiefly in the Treaty of Frankfurt of 1871 which was imposed on France after the Franco-Prussian war. It facilitated and represented the formation of a powerful German nation in the centre of Europe, leaving France poorer by an indemnity of five billion francs, humiliated and vengeful, and believing that the two lost provinces of Alsace and Lorraine could be recovered only by force of arms. Nor was the resentment towards the victors lessened among nationalistic Frenchmen in the succeeding years. They saw the German Chancellor, Bismarck, bind together the powers in such a way as to isolate France. In 1879 he concluded the Dual Alliance with Austria which was to last through to the first world war. Under it, German support was promised for Austria-Hungary in the event of a Russian invasion, in return for Austro-Hungarian neutrality in a Franco-German conflict. The German government did not promise support if the Dual Monarchy were to provoke a war against Russia and there was no associated military understanding. Being defensive, it was no obstacle to the conclusion of an alliance that bound Russia together with the two central powers in the Three Emperors' League of 1881 for mutual defence against aggression by any fourth power. Bismarck thus used the skills of diplomacy to redress the rigidities of political geography; the difficulties of Germany's central position in Europe which might have condemned her to fighting a two-front war had been overcome by the securing of her eastern frontier and the isolation of France.

In 1882 the alliance of the two central powers was supplemented by a Triple Alliance under which Italy promised to help Germany in case of a French invasion in return for the help of Germany and Austria-Hungary if she were herself invaded. There was a further provision that if two or more powers attacked one of the allies without direct provocation, all would fight. It was on the basis that this direct provocation was lacking that Italy did not join the war in 1914 with her two allies. Still the Triple Alliance was part of the furniture of the European diplomatic stage for over thirty years. The possibility of the three powers acting together had to be reckoned with by the governments of Europe in shaping their foreign policy. The secrecy of some of the provisions of these treaties made for uncertainty, for each time one of these diplomatic icebergs floated into view all the talk among diplomats was of the part below the surface.

This complicated and secret pattern of alliances was not static. Not only were their provisions reviewed from time to time but they were altered by the varying alignments of the powers. The agreements followed the interests of the participants and derived their strength from the importance which the powers attached to these documents; treaties, like currency, could lose value over time. Germany had, firstly, some difficulty in reconciling her connection with both Austria-Hungary and Russia, for those two powers had an obvious and continuing difference of interest concerning the Balkans, where Bismarck tried to keep both states in the German camp. After he fell from power, his successors showed less concern for the wooing of Russia. Still, the signs were already there that France and Russia would draw together. The new German rulers placed too much reliance on the difference in political outlook between the ruling groups in Russia and France: the one an autocracy, the other a republic, the one with revolutionary experience as recently as 1871, the other with a dread of revolution. On the German side, Bismarck had sensed the danger and in 1887 had concluded a secret Reinsurance Treaty with Russia which, in effect, meant that Russia would remain neutral in a Franco-German war and Germany remain neutral in an Austro-Russian war, except when either of the signatories launched the conflict. Still, in the same year the Russian government raised a 500 million franc loan on the French money market and Russian industrialisation was largely supported by French money.

In France, the newly emerging pattern in international relations was seen very clearly and supported by a young journalist and deputy in the Chamber, Théophile Delcassé. When the drawing together of Russia and France was symbolised by the French fleet visiting the Russian naval base of Kronstadt, he wrote to his wife: 'For a long time no one, or almost no one, was willing to believe in the Franco-Russian entente. And yet it was not difficult to see that it was inevitable. A glance at the map was enough.' Delcassé had been born at Pamiers near the Spanish frontier in 1832. His earliest memories of international affairs were of a France triumphant during the war of Italian unification and his more recent memories of a

Fig. 1 – *Waving the Flag.* The Empire Day Parade in Hyde Park, London, 1913. In the cadet review the salute was taken by Lord Roberts, the most eminent British soldier, and sixty-four colonial and dominion flags were carried.

Fig. 2 – *Men-of-war.* A line of dreadnoughts photographed from *H.M.S. Superb.* The giant tripod mast was designed to provide a vibration-free platform aloft during the firing of the twelve-inch guns.

Fig. 3 – *Strengthening the Entente.* A Punch cartoon of April 1905 neatly suggests the way in which the German intervention helped transform an agreement on colonial issues into something more.

Fig. 4 – *The Internal Conflict. (Left)* A general railway strike in August 1911 paralysed the industrial north of England. Troops were called in, killing two of the strikers before a settlement was negotiated. Liverpool was one of the centres of unrest and here police remove a prisoner to the station. *(Right)* A suffragette who tried to force her way into Buckingham Palace with Mrs Pankhurst and many others in May 1914 is arrested by two of the two thousand police who defended the Palace.

Fig. 5 – *Sarajevo.* The Archduke Francis Ferdinand drove down the Appel Quay where he survived a bomb attempt, the culprit having to be removed from the Miljata River. After an official welcome at the Town Hall (marked with a cross) the Archduke was driven back down the Quay, only to be shot at the corner of Franz Joseph street.

France humiliated by Germany. These public events perhaps reinforced two tendencies derived from an unhappy childhood with a stepmother lacking affection: one was secrecy, and the other the overflowing of his personal emotions into intense patriotism. 'My objective,' he wrote, 'is the resurrection of the country.' Hence, after a successful career in journalism, he entered the Chamber as a Republican and made a triumphantly patriotic maiden speech. He retained, however, a constant anxiety about his own abilities although their extent became very soon obvious. He shared with his countrymen a distrust of the Germans and a devotion to the provinces lost to France in 1871, Alsace-Lorraine, a subject on which he was so sensitive that his children never felt that they could bring themselves to speak of it in the house.

In January 1894 the Franco-Russian alliance was concluded. The two governments exchanged guarantees against the possibility of German aggression and agreed to mobilise their forces if any of the Triple Alliance powers mobilised theirs, thus putting them on a war footing. The importance of mobilisation was pinpointed by the French Chief of Staff: '. . . to allow a million men to mobilise on one's frontiers without at once doing the same is to forfeit all possibility of following suit, to put oneself in the position of an individual with a pistol in his pocket who allows his neighbour to point a weapon at his head without reaching for his own.' The pattern was now set, the Triple Alliance on one side and the Dual Alliance on the other; both were somewhat leaky vessels but the alignment was to become more fixed with the passing years.

ORIGINS OF THE ENTENTE CORDIALE

Delcassé would have been glad to enter into an understanding with Britain, but the major obstacle to be surmounted was the British occupation of Egypt. The dimensions of the problem became more obvious to him after his appointment as under-secretary for the colonies in 1893. He quickly formulated a plan for an expedition to Fashoda on the upper Nile with the intention not so much of winning Egyptian territory as of forcing the British to end their temporary occupation which had started eleven years before. For the British, withdrawal from Egypt might, through the establishment of Egyptian nationalist or foreign influence, threaten the security of the Suez canal. The importance of the canal to the British electorate was even greater than the proportion of British trade it carried (perhaps 16%) would suggest. The French government saw the matter more in relation to their traditional position of strength in the Mediterranean, but was throughout heavily influenced by a small number of strategically placed colonial enthusiasts. The first French expedition to

Fashoda was unsuccessful, but the Cabinet agreed to the despatch of a second after Delcassé's fall from office in 1895 although its probable results do not seem to have been discussed. The occupation of the upper Nile by the French would have opened to them the opportunity of interfering with the flow of the Nile which was Egypt's life-line, its annual flooding providing fertility for its parched soil. This second expedition under Captain Marchand eventually arrived at Fashoda, provoking a crisis which was the first major business for Delcassé in his new role of Foreign Secretary. The British government had already indicated its determination to resist any intrusion into the Southern Sudan, which Sir Herbert Kitchener was engaged in conquering. Kitchener and Marchand confronted one another at Fashoda in 1898 in one of the great set pieces of the imperial age. The balance of force lay with Kitchener, and Delcassé ordered Marchand's withdrawal in November. Britain rejoiced. With a taste characteristic of high imperialism, the City of London presented Kitchener with a sword of honour with gold bands, diamonds, rubies and the hilt decorated with figures of justice, Britannia, etc.

Despite this tense confrontation, even before Kitchener went to Fashoda the French Colonial Party (a collection of pressure groups) had started to suggest a compromise over Egypt. Their proposal was to exchange a recognition of British predominance in Egypt for French predominance in Morocco. This plan was gradually adopted by Delcasse and became the foundation for the Anglo-French entente of 1904.

As in the case of the Franco-Russian alliance of 1894, the German government had tended to assume that the traditional enmity between the French and the British people would thrive on the continual colonial friction of which the Fashoda incident was but one example. Thus there was some surprise in German government circles when it proved possible to reach accord on a list of outstanding points at issue, even on such ancient arguments as the dispute over Newfoundland fishing rights which had provided steady business for the British Foreign Office over two centuries. The central point was the agreement of April 1904 consisting primarily of an exchange of British predominance in Egypt for French predominance in Morocco, with provisions to protect the British naval position in the western Mediterranean. Perhaps we should not give to the Entente Cordiale the resilience that it proved to have in 1914, but the agreement, which was plainly a prelude to co-operation within Europe, needs explanation.

It is an interesting demonstration of the way in which the world was shrinking that an event as seemingly distant as the Anglo-Japanese alliance of 1902 had its part in making the Entente. This alliance was directed at the containment of Russia in Asia and was partly a naval engagement by which both powers secretly agreed to maintain their naval forces up to the level of the next naval power in the area, that is, Russia. To that extent it was a step taken to help leave the Royal Navy free to concentrate its forces more in home waters if necessary. It provided a precedent by which the British government, which had previously remained aloof from alliances, could engage itself in commitments abroad. It posed a particular problem for Delcassé, however, for France was bound by alliance to Russia while Britain was now bound to Japan. There was much evidence that a Russo-Japanese war was imminent and it remained possible that the powers on either side of the English channel would be brought into the conflict, hence the urgency for agreement grew greater.

The German government itself made perhaps the largest contribution to the formation of the Entente for it rebuffed somewhat hesitant offers of co-operation that came from both Britain and France at the turn of the century. British public opinion was influenced also by the industrial rivalry between the two powers and the obvious intent of the German navy as a threat to Britain. It was, however, the Moroccan crisis of 1905 which changed the Entente from a limited colonial agreement into a major element in the European balance. From the first, the German Foreign ministry had been concerned that Britain and France should try to reach an agreement without consulting Germany. There was therefore prestige to be considered and there was also the importance of Morocco itself, one of the few countries in which Germany could still trade freely in a world increasingly closed by high tariff barriers. The 1904 agreement between France and Britain, while nominally upholding the position of the Sultan, in secret provisions prepared for the partition of the country between Spain and France. A strong public gesture was needed so that it might become clear to the French government that it could neither settle Morocco nor secure permanent diplomatic advantage without Germany. On 31 March 1905 the Kaiser landed from his yacht at Tangier, spoke in favour of the independence of the Sultan, and called for free access to Morocco for all nations – that is, there should be no special commercial or political advantages for France. This dramatic statement was a clear manifestation of the Kaiser's private attitude: 'As to France, we know the road to Paris and we can get there again if needs be. They should remember no fleet can defend Paris.'

The German government called for an international conference which would not, it was convinced, sustain the French position in Morocco but would secure Germany an easy diplomatic victory. The unwillingness and inability of the British and Russian governments to support their ally would, the Germans thought, become apparent and the Entente would be destroyed. The French government was divided on the line it should take towards Germany. Rouvier, the Premier, was impressed with the weakness of French defences and was inclined to co-operate with the Germans; he therefore attempted to reach an understanding with the German government, behind his Foreign Secretary's back, by indicating a readiness to dismiss Delcassé. Meanwhile, Delcassé sat in his office reading the German report of these top-secret negotiations, for the Ministry had broken the German code, a piece of good fortune so important that he was, ironically enough, unable to reveal his knowledge. The German desire to remove Delcassé was of a piece with their general policy of showing the French people the need for dependence on Germany, but more importantly it derived from a desire to rid themselves of a known opponent who refused to offer them important concessions over Morocco. Delcassé was also pursuing another highly successful policy which endangered German interests. The long expected Russo-Japanese war had broken out in February 1904 and the French government was well placed to help the Russians by mediating a settlement of the war which, with the heavy Russian defeats, each day brought the overthrow of Tsarist government closer. Such a mediation would, in the view of the German Chancellor Bülow, lead directly to a Russian-French-British alliance inimical to German interests. Hence, under threat of German attack, Rouvier was induced to dismiss Delcassé on 6 June 1905. The decision was welcomed with relief by the French press, but the applause died away as it became obvious that the Germans would make no concession. Having called for a conference, they could not enter into separate negotiations with France and thought to gain a diplomatic triumph at the conference which met at Algeciras in Morocco in January 1906.

There were now new elements in the situation. A Liberal government had replaced the Conservatives in Britain and Sir Edward Grey was the new Foreign Secretary. He, however, maintained continuity of policy and saw support of the Anglo-French entente as a cardinal point of British policy, so the more obdurate the German government, the stronger Grey's support of France, for it would never do to allow German predominance on the continent. He was influenced by the British dependence on Germany in relation to Egypt especially, which had struck him forcibly when he had been at the Foreign Office 1892-5. In the intervening years, the German exploitation of Britain's South African difficulties (the Jameson Raid 1896 and the Anglo-Boer War 1899-1902) and the wider commercial and naval rivalry reinforced his suspicion of German designs. He had, therefore, approved of the Entente and now in Office did his best to sustain it, not only by ample and successful diplomatic backing at Algeciras but also by giving official standing to the conversations that started on 1 January between military officers of the two countries. The conversations were based on the assumption of a British intervention on the continent in the event of a German invasion.

There were two chief issues involved in the conference: reforms in the internal administration of Morocco, especially in relation to the police, and the recognition of the French government's having a special position in the country because of her role in neighbouring Algeria. France did not get all it wanted on either of these points, the police were to remain under the Sultan but have also the surveillance of the diplomats in Morocco, and Morocco continued to be regarded as an international question. But the German success – and it was limited – was bought dearly, for Germany found itself at the conference with only the partial support of one nation, Austria-Hungary, while its tactics threw Britain and Franch closer together than before and helped win French public opinion for the Entente.

THE ANGLO-RUSSIAN ENTENTE

The completion of the Entente by the creation of links between Britain and Russia had been in Grey's mind before he came to office. He saw it then as a chance to control 'our worst enemy and our greatest danger', Germany. For Britain such an agreement offered the chance of absolute security, a goal as elusive as it was dangerous. The Russian government, still nursing its wounds from defeat in Asia, saw such an understanding as helping to restore its European status. It was turning its foreign policy again towards control of the Straits which were important strategically for fleet access to the Mediterranean and commercially as an outlet for south Russian wheat. In that area co-operation with Germany seemed remote because of its increasing influence in Turkey. Nor did another Russian ambition, enlarged influence in the Balkans, offer chances of agreement with Germany for there conflict existed with Austria-Hungary and the Germans could hardly be expected to sacrifice the interests of their most dependable ally.

Anglo-Russian negotiations, opening in St Petersburg in May 1906, were not concluded until August 1907. The problems to be overcome were great and the agreement correspondingly limited; that it was reached at all was evidence of the single-minded purpose of Grey and Sir Charles Hardinge, ambassador to St Petersburg. From the British point of view the long existing Russian threat to India had to be laid to rest and the agreement contributed by recognising Afghanistan as a British sphere of influence and Tibet as independent under Chinese suzerainty. The substance of the matter lay, however, in a demarcation of spheres in Persia. Here again, as in Morocco, the European powers were engaged in competitive exploitation of a developing country. Russia had the predominant position, especially in the north, and used the Shah's constant need for loans to extend its influence through banking, insurance, shipping and road building. The Persian army was trained by Russian officers. In the south, and especially on the Persian gulf, the British presence was very obvious; it yielded commercial benefits but also had great strategic significance for the defence of India. The rivalry had a long history but two new components in the situation pushed the two competitors together. First, a German-backed group secured a concession in 1899 to construct a railway from Constantinople to the Persian Gulf. In fact, it did not get far, but the prospect of such a line tapping the middle eastern trade, because of the possibility of branch lines drawing off the Persian trade, alarmed Russia. Secondly, the Russian defeat in the war with Japan made desirable a settlement of outstanding issues with Britain. While Japan and Britain remained in alliance as enemies of Russia, argued Izvolsky the Foreign Secretary, then Russia would always be looking over her shoulder to the east and hence unable to exert the influence of a major power in Europe. Grey, likewise looked to Europe and saw the opportunity of settling the long standing threat to India's northern frontier. That would enable greater concentration on Europe and by lessening this dispute would make for an easier co-operation of the three anti-German powers. The Persian agreement cannot be said to have been popular in either country; 'a regrettable alliance between the sand dune and the sea' was one later description. It ignored the deep conflict of interests between the two nations. The Persian government, which had secured some measure of independence by playing off the two powers, were bitterly critical, especially of the British who had shown some sympathy for the movement among Persians towards greater independence and a more constitutional form of government.

THE ANNEXATION OF BOSNIA-HERZEGOVINA

At the time of the Anglo-Russian Convention the British government also promised to examine Russian proposals on the Straits. The British found it impossible to agree to those, so Izvolsky looked towards co-operation with Austria-Hungary. Here there was the basis of a bargain, for each had the power to help the other with pressing problems – Austria-Hungary could aid the Russian desire to win control of the Straits, and Russia could aid Austro-Hungarian ambitions in the Balkans. The former arose from the increasing importance of the Straits as the door through which passed so much Russian trade (87.2% of wheat exports, 1901-1910), the latter from the dual monarchy's desire to resist Slav, especially Serbian, nationalism. In July 1908 Izvolsky, the Russian foreign minister proposed just such an agreement to the Austro-Hungarian government and later in the year entered into secret negotiations with his opposite number. When, however, the Dual Monarchy annexed Bosnia-Herzegovina in October, public anger in Russia was directed against Izvolsky. The opponents of the plan, who included the Prime Minister Stolypin, looked forward to a Turko-Slavic confederation in the Balkans and in the short term pressed for a conference of the powers to discuss the annexation. Such a policy would have worked if Russia's allies were as willing to support her in the Balkans as were the Germans to support Austria-Hungary. But it was a far more important issue for the German government than for the British or French. There was, first of all, the memory of the disastrous result of the last conference of the powers; Algeciras was not a precedent to be followed. Secondly, Austria was Germany's only reliable ally and, as Bülow, the Chancellor, said 'her humiliation would be our humiliation'; German prestige in Europe had to be protected. Thirdly, a diplomatic victory for Germany, that is European acceptance of the annexation, would break the ring of encircling powers. The French, Bülow thought, would not be prepared to go to war over the Balkans and their saying as much to the Russian government would shatter the strength of their alliance. Hence, both in diplomacy and military preparations the German government gave Austria its fullest support. The chiefs of staff of the two countries exchanged letters which, although including few precise arrangements, had the effect of changing the dual alliance into an offensive agreement. If Austria attacked Serbia and Russia mobilised, (as happened in 1914) then Germany would mobilise and, under the inflexible character of the German military plans, that meant war. In diplomacy, too, the German backing for Austria was thorough, indeed more thorough than was required. In March 1909 when the annexation issue was already close to a negotiated settlement, Bülow threatened the Russian government that, if they did not accept the annexation immediately and unequivocally, Germany would 'let things take their course', which implied an Austrian invasion of Serbia and all that would follow from that. The Russian government, ready neither militarily nor diplomatically for war,acquiesced in the German demand and Britain and France followed suit in accepting the Austrian annexation without a conference.

On the surface it seemed a noteworthy German success but in fact it strengthened European suspicion of German intentions. The Russian Ambassador to Paris was not alone in drawing the conclusion: '. . . if military measures are already prepared in time of peace, diplomatic questions may be solved by threats and the exercise of strong pressure.'

3. MILITARISM

One of the characteristics of the pre-war years in Europe was labelled by contemporaries *militarism.* As with many another 'ism' this had a cluster of meanings around a central core which was, in this case, the observable tendency to regard military efficiency as a permanent aim of the state. The word seems to have come into the English language in the 1860 s and became very quickly linked with Prussia, which was hardly surprising, considering the impact of the defeat of Austria in 1866. Militarism was not, however, confined to Prussia and other nations began to emulate the presumed advantage of having a large standing army. Once that principle was accepted, simple population growth tended to make for larger armies, but as can be seen from the table below, a higher proportion, as well as a greater number, of young men were drawn into the army, so that in some cases such as France, the army grew far faster than the population.

Standing Armies and Population – Selected Countries 1880-1914

	France		*Germany*		*Austria-Hungary*		*Russia*	
	Army (thou)	**Pop (mill)**	**A (thou)**	**P (mill)**	**A (thou)**	**P (mill)**	**A (thou)**	**P (mill)**
1880	503	39.2	419	40.2	240	37.8	766	97.7
1890	502	40.0	487	44.2	337	–	647	–
1900	673	40.7	495	50.6	375	47	1119	131.7
1910	713	41.5	636	58.5	410	51.4	1225	153.8
1914	846		812		424		1300	

Such increases in army size are made up of a great many separate decisions taken over the decades before outbreak of war in 1914, but one can speculate on the general causes for such growth: the wider acceptance of ideas sympathetic to military thinking, the notion of struggle in society, and obviously the recurrent crises which bred a sense of political uncertainty, although these crises were both cause and effect for, as in the case of the Bosnian annexation, the apparent success of diplomacy backed by 'the pistol in the pocket' stepped up military preparations and hence fostered further uncertainty and further crises.

WAR PLANS

An important part of the growth of armies and a further strengthening of the tendency to regard military efficiency as a paramount state aim came from the development of military organisation and planning. The Prussian victory of 1866, the start of much military thinking, pointed to the need for an army to have a 'brain', that is, a general staff to utilise intelligence reports, formulate mobilisation schemes and draw up plans for war. As the numbers of soldiers who had to be mobilised increased so the importance of railways became greater, for speed was essential, so Europe started to move in the direction of the war by time-table. The more preparations which were required, the earlier the beginning of the count-down for war.

War planning only gradually achieved the menace it possessed in the last years before the war. By the mid-nineties, it is true, Count von Schlieffen, German Chief of Staff, had formulated the basic features of the plan associated with his name. Because of the drawing together of Russia and France, Germany, he reasoned, would have to contemplate the possibility of war on both the eastern and western fronts. Since the Russian army, because of size and distances involved, would take so long to mobilise, he planned for a quick victory on the western front executed by the bulk of the German forces, and then a turn east. At this time the French war plan was defensive-offensive; it was based on the belief that the Germans might be induced to attack through two gaps left in the otherwise formidable French frontier defences and once that occurred French forces would be ready to launch a massive counter-attack. British war planning was not in this league. After fruitless attempts to co-ordinate the planning of the services chiefs in the shooting season, Lord Rosebery, Foreign Secretary in 1893, commented: 'I think they care more for grouse than for the Empire.' There was, of course, a deep distrust of planning which was thought likely to lead to war, so the sum total of British plans for war with France and Russia (the most likely enemies) consisted of only two pages.

With the passing years war planning became more threatening. The Schlieffen plan took an altogether new aspect for, as formulated in December 1905, it involved the violation of neutral territory (Belgium and Holland) in order to strike at France with a great wheeling advance that would bring German troops around Paris without the difficulty of facing the close fortifications of the French eastern frontier. That is the first important feature of the plan. It involved the breach of neutrality and would therefore put the German government in the wrong. That was known to successive German Chancellors but they did not prevent it. Because of the breadth of the Belgian front and the need to capture its railway system as the link between the German and French, the greater

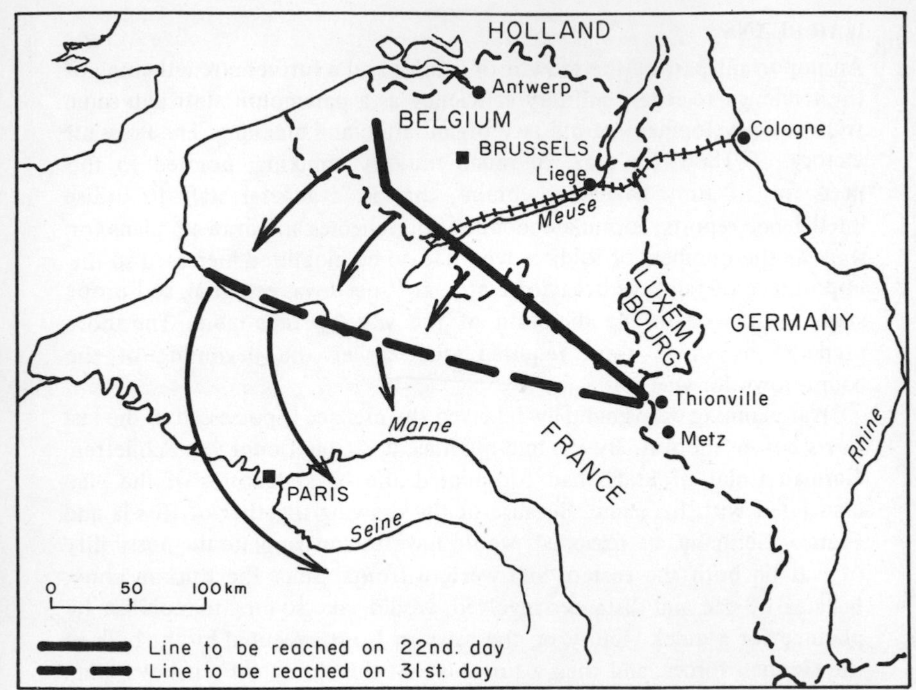

The Schlieffen Plan

part of the German army in the west would have to be deployed on this right wing. The insistence on a strong right wing is the second major feature of the plan and it entailed therefore a weak left wing in the south, but the subtlety of the plan was that, on the principle of a revolving door, the harder the French pushed in the south the easier would be the task of the German right in outflanking them.

Moltke, nephew of the great victor of the Franco-Prussian war, took over from Schlieffen as Chief of Staff in 1905. He retained the main features of the Schlieffen plan while, however, modifying it in a way that reduced still further its chances of success. He decided that it was preferable not to cross Dutch territory because a neutral Holland might provide a useful route for supplies and would remove the dangers of having an enemy in the rear of advancing German forces. This decision, however, narrowed the gap through which German forces could advance and made the early possession of Liège, which covered the key Meuse railway, an essential part of mobilisation. Thus on the third day part of Belgium was to be seized, a part of the programme which raised a host of diplomatic difficulties regarding the violation of neutrality and the declaration of war. Schlieffen's plan put Germany in the wrong at the outset of war: Moltke's plan did so even before war was declared. Moltke's second major change in the Schlieffen plan struck at the rationale behind it; he changed the relative strength of the right and left wings of the German army in the west. We can see why; the German forces in the south were pitifully small and made to appear more so as French military planning started to take account of the mood of offence prevalent in army circles. Schlieffen's dying words in 1912 are said to have been 'See you make the right wing strong'; Moltke did not, thus reducing still further whatever chances of success the plan had.

The implications of the plan were very important. Although war could come from the east, the mobilisation had to be directed primarily against France. The plan was inflexible so mobilisation meant war and meant, too, the violation of Belgian neutrality, an action very likely to bring Britain into the conflict.

At about the same time as Schlieffen was giving his plan its final form (in late 1905), Anglo-French military conversations began. These were a product of the French wish to give greater substance to an entente much under pressure from the Moroccan crisis. War planning of any kind was alien to the Liberal tradition; concerted planning of this kind which went forward on the assumption of British support for France in the event of an invasion, was unheard of. Grey intended that it should remain unheard of for although Grey authorised official talks from New Year's day 1906, Campbell-Bannerman, the Prime Minister, was not told until the end of the month. Campbell-Bannerman perceived their importance: 'It comes very close to an honourable undertaking and will soon be well known on both sides of the Rhine'. Despite subsequent attempts to play down the importance of the talks, they aligned Britain very much with France and made an Anglo-German understanding far more difficult. The technical importance of the talks quickly grew. 'Soldiers in peace-time', it has been remarked, 'are as useful as chimneys in summer' and, having already engaged in some unofficial discussions in 1905 they seized the new sense of purpose given them by these talks. The token force contemplated in 1906 flowered to become the five divisions sent across the channel by the British army in 1914, partly due to careful cultivation by the British Director of Military Operations, Sir Henry Wilson.

French military planning underwent many revisions before the war, showing the impact of that school of thought that stressed the value of attack. The justification for belief in the virtues of the offensive were only partly military, as it also reflected the ideas of the time, being a military application of Bergson's *Elan Vital,* i.e. a tremendous drive or instinct that could overcome all opposition. The thinking of the school headed by Ferdinand Foch is represented in this maxim of his prize pupil, Colonel de Grandmaison: 'All attacks are to be pressed to the extreme . . . to charge the enemy with the bayonet in order to destroy him . . . . This result can only be obtained at the price of bloody sacrifice. Any other conception ought to be rejected as contrary to the very nature of war.'

To an extent this was the negation of planning and Foch took the view that the plans should remain in his head rather than on paper. The planning that was on paper involved a two pronged offensive in Alsace-Lorraine passing north and south of the Thionville-Metz area with two French armies available to shift westwards if the German army should break the neutrality of Belgium.

Having drawn up detailed military plans for the outbreak of war, it is natural that those concerned should reflect on the most convenient time for it. If in addition it was held that war was inevitable, or indeed desirable, then the question of timing became crucial. For some years before the war the question that posed itself for many of the ruling elites in Europe was not 'War or Peace'? but rather 'War now or War later'? Once the question of timing became so important the advice of the military experts loomed larger. In Germany in December 1912 the Kaiser raised the matter with his advisers and Admiral Tirpitz, head of the navy, asked for an eighteen month postponement of war to allow time for the widening of the Kiel Canal so that the larger German warships had easy access to the North Sea. In the following spring Foch told the British Director of Military Operations, Sir Henry Wilson, that the French favoured no long postponement of general war because if it came soon it would be a Balkan war and hence Russian co-operation could be relied upon. In 1913, also, the French government lengthened the period of conscription for military service from two years to three, thus effectively strengthening the army. The Russian and German governments both took steps to strengthen their armies in the same year.

There was, of course, a time lag between drafting further men into the army and increasing the number of trained soldiers. Moltke recognised that Germany was in a better position to fight in mid-1914 than she would be later and it is interesting to note that he approached Jagow, German foreign secretary and asked him in May or June to provoke a war.

Shortly before, Colonel House, President Wilson's emissary, reported to his chief:

> The situation is extraordinary. It is militarism run stark mad. Unless someone acting for you can bring about a different understanding, there is some day to be an awful cataclysm. No one in Europe can do it. There is too much hatred, too many jealousies. Whenever England consents, France and Russia will close in on Germany and Austria.

NAVAL GROWTH

Nor was it only the armies that expanded in these years. The process of growth can be illustrated by the navies. In 1889 the British government adopted the two-power standard, the criterion that the Royal Navy should be equal in size to its two nearest rivals. The new ship building that this caused was supplemented by a further naval construction programme in 1894. It was a sign of the times that Liberals, so long identified with peace and retrenchment, should have initiated such a programme. Gladstone, now an old man with failing eyesight, resigned rather than put through the programme, complaining to his Cabinet of what he called 'accursed militarism'. The German naval laws of 1898 and 1900 were directed at Britain and were the work of Admiral Tirpitz, German minister of marine and were fostered by the Kaiser's continuing interest, an interest that went down even to the details of war-ship construction. The second naval law provided for thirty-eight battleships to be built over twenty years. It was to be a force large enough to challenge the British Home fleet and increase Germany's attractiveness as an ally.

A new twist was given to this Anglo-German rivalry by the appointment of Admiral Sir John Fisher as service head of the Royal Navy, First Sea Lord, in 1903. Fisher at sixty-two had behind him a long naval career marked by a single-minded intensity of purpose and an assurance of being right, combined with a candour and extravagance that perhaps made him seem more war-like than he was. He soon became an object of fear for many inhabitants of the north German ports who nursed a suspicion that he might launch an unannounced attack destroying the German war fleet in home waters before the outbreak of war. He certainly contemplated such a step on at least two occasions. More serious than Fisher's musings were the steps he took to put the Royal Navy in readiness to meet the German threat. The warships which had been dispersed about the world acting as a maritime peace-keeping or war-making force were reduced in number and concentrated nearer to Britain. At the same time vessels were made ready for service by the provision of the nucleus of a crew ready for easy expansion in the event of war. The message of this concentration of strength in the North Sea was not lost on the German navy.

Technology, the skills of the industrial societies, was also put in the service of the arms rivalries. That is exemplified by the construction of the Dreadnought, a new type of warship the first of which was launched in 1906. Fisher claimed that the Dreadnought was the equivalent of two-and-one-half of the old style battleships. Their concentration on all big-guns (ten 12 inch) and high speed (21 knots) revolutionised warship design, giving them a decisive advantage in dealing with the predominantly smaller guns of previous warships. The advent of new style vessels, and it was new battlecruisers as well as dreadnoughts that the Royal Navy was busy securing, rendered the older vessels out of date much as a new model car reduces the value of the old. A contemporary remarked that the British 'had started the competition in arms on an entirely new basis upon terms of advantage.' The German reaction was delayed, but came finally with the naval law of 1908 which involved the laying down of four new dreadnought-style battleships in the following years. A heated debate occurred within the British government with the Admiralty calling for six new dreadnoughts to be laid down and others urging that four was sufficient. The comparison of the relative strength of fleets allowed ample room for argument: should one compare total naval strength or vessels in commission? What relative weight should one give to submarines? How does one compare different classes of warship? How are vessels stationed in the North Sea to be rated against those stationed in the Pacific? Even presuming some agreement could be reached on the way in which the navies could be compared, there still remained the question of justification. There was a notion that a country of a certain importance with certain overseas possessions and trade was justified in having a navy of a certain size. This allowed ample room for argument, especially when Germany had the most formidable of the continental armies.

The debate over whether Britain should lay down four or six dreadnoughts was extended into the public arena where the difficulties of making comparisons were compounded by the ignorance of the disputants. The compromise arrived at by the Cabinet, four in 1909 and four in 1910, was overturned by public opinion which demanded 'We want eight and we won't wait', so construction started on eight dreadnoughts in 1909. The public, or at least the vocal section of it, had not arrived at its decision unaided. 'Anxiety, not a sense of security, lies at the root of readiness' wrote Lord Esher, a prominent British defence expert, to Fisher, who scarcely needed to be told, 'An invasion scare is the mill of God which grinds you out a navy of dreadnoughts and keeps the British people war-like in spirit'. Esher and Fisher were among those who contributed to the formulation of just such an invasion scare as had preceded previous naval enlargements. New organisations preached the need of a larger navy and old organisations strenuously supported them, letters were written, speeches delivered, questions asked in Parliament, information was secretly provided for the newspapers from serving naval officers and the Conservative Opposition cashed in. They raised the prospect of Germany having, by 1911, some 21 to 25 battleships. In fact in 1911 they had six and a year later nine. In part a political manoeuvre, in part a concern for defence mixed with varying degrees of self-interest, the naval scare of 1909 played on and heightened English fears of Germany. These were partly military but also commercial: the sneaking suspicion that German yards could build warships faster and more efficiently than British yards was representative of a wider economic antagonism.

The Anglo-German naval rivalry, exacerbated by the British new construction, took a further turn for the worse in 1912. Alarmed at the proximity of war during the Agadir crisis, the British Liberal government was pressed by its own supporters to attempt some understanding with Germany. Limitation on arms would allow more room for expenditure on measures to make the bulk of the people's lives more bearable, so a German-speaking Cabinet minister, Lord Haldane, was sent to Berlin in February 1912. Amongst his tasks was the attempt to reduce the proposed German naval expansion. According to the naval law of 1900, Germany was now due to shift from constructing four new battleships *per annum* to building two. Such a reduction was unacceptable to Tirpitz and the draft law proposed that three be built each year to 1917 and that the number of personnel be increased so that more vessels might be commissioned, so that nearly four-fifths of the entire navy could be in a state of war readiness. The Haldane mission came to nothing, partly because the British Foreign Office was exceedingly reluctant to take any action that would endanger the Entente, while the German government, even when it would consider modifying the naval law, would only do so in exchange for a promise of British neutrality if either power were engaged in a defensive war.

The Anglo-German naval rivalry had reached stalemate and remained there through to the war. The problem illustrates the way in which the needs of the diplomats and of the service chiefs interacted: a hearty wish to see the Haldane mission fail was shared by Bertie, the British Ambassador in Paris, Nicolson, the head of the British Foreign Office, and Tirpitz in Berlin. Any warmth between London and Berlin cast a chill over the Entente. Moreover, any negotiations over naval reductions might raise the awkward question of dreadnoughts built or proposed at colonial expense (the *New Zealand* amongst others) and not included as British vessels in the comparisons. The Kaiser, very much subject to navy influence, showed little inclination to make concessions for the sake of a broader political understanding, and in 1912, Winston Churchill, now in charge of the Admiralty, took the policy of concentration still further, removing British warships even from that traditional centre of British naval power, the Mediterranean. A naval convention was concluded with the French government in November 1912 that left it principal responsibility for the defence of the Mediterranean as the Admiralty had to reckon on the possibility of facing the Austrian and Italian dreadnoughts built and building. The needs of strategy strengthened still further the bonds of the Entente.

4. INTERNAL CAUSES OF WAR

Another vantage point from which to study the coming of war is the internal politics of the participating countries. It is not unreasonable to suggest that the statesmen who made the decisions which led to war had one eye, if not both, on the situation in their own country; some political considerations might have made militarism and an aggressive foreign policy seem desirable. Such policies might, for example, reunite a divided nation under the banner of patriotism and fix the existing leadership more firmly in power. Again, external success through war or a dangerous political manoeuvre might divert attention from grievances at home. This is not to say that home politics did not offer very good reasons for avoiding war. The lesson of the 1905 revolution in Russia, brought on by war, was not quickly forgotten there or elsewhere. Sir Edward Grey, the British Foreign Secretary, thought that 'the next country, if any, which had a great and successful war, unless it were purely a war of defence against aggression, would be the first to have a social revolution.' He admitted, however, that industrial troubles, such as strikes, might be suspended at the outbreak of war. Although opinions divided, there was a great deal of speculation in high political circles in Europe on the connection between international and internal tensions, both of which were widespread in these years. Certainly Britain had her share: there was high unemployment and severe industrial unrest in the pre-war years. If the war between the sexes was perennial at least at this time it broke into open conflict with suffragettes besieging the male citadels of power. In 1914 Britain was close to civil war: in Ireland the Ulster Volunteers were drilling, determined to resist the Liberal government's wish to grant Home Rule to all Ireland, and Bonar Law, the leader of the Conservative Opposition, had made plain his sympathy with them in taking arms against the government. The coming of war allowed the Liberals to put the bill to create a Home Rule parliament in Dublin into cold storage.

In France also, these years saw severe internal disorder. Opinion was very divided not only on the rights and wrongs of strikes but also by the so-called National Revival. At the time of the Dreyfus case the army and conservative parties and groups in society had been discredited; they had been associated with those who imprisoned Dreyfus and when he was cleared of all suspicion they suffered a setback in public standing. The National Revival was a rediscovery, largely in conservative newspapers, of the patriotic fervour that had been the chief hallmark of these groups at that time. This revival, so marked after 1911, came not so much from the Agadir incident and anti-German feeling, as from internal politics. The conservative parties in France, usually divided, found a core for agreement in attacks upon the anti-militarism of the Radicals and Socialists. The situation of the Dreyfus affair was now reversed: it was the turn of the left-wing parties to be discredited by the use of national and military sentiment, as also by the use of what was termed national discipline, that is, strict control of strikes. This is seen clearly when, in 1913, the debates occurred in the Chamber on the bill to re-introduce three year military training. The Chamber divided not so much on clear party lines as on exactly the same lines as divided it on anti-union laws; that is, the Deputies who favoured a strong line against strikes also favoured a three year military training. They formed a unit and one large enough to ensure conservative governments. Conservative elements exploited the issue of the supposed German threat to defeat left wing parties. Peace-makers, real or apparent, are not always blessed, at least in politics, for conservative parties having taken the national flag for themselves were able to attack those who opposed militarism as being careless of the interests of the nation. Socialists particularly, since they advocated a general strike by workers, were in an exposed position. They believed that the enemy was a class-enemy and was within each country: workers should, without respect for national boundaries, be united in their efforts to build a better society. There were a minority of socialists who were more concerned with the prospects of revolution emerging from war, but under Jean Jaurès most French socialists followed their leader in seeing opposition to militarism as one of their main goals and for many on the left the means to be used was the general strike. A strike by all workers would, it was claimed, paralyse the war effort and ensure the maintenance of peace.

In 1913-14 there was a distinct revival of industrial and political unrest in Germany. The economy had entered a recession in late 1912, industrial unemployment in 1913 was 2.9% and rose to 3.2% in the first six months of 1914. Politically, Germany had reached stalemate. The Social Democrats had become, in the 1912 election, the largest party in the Reichstag but found their long awaited victory rather hollow. No new social legislation was enacted and the reform of the Prussian franchise, the main object of their labour, made no progress. Prussia dominated Germany and without change in Prussia the Social Democrats could make no substantial progress. There was not even the prospect of taking a strong line against militarism. The desire to do so was much lessened by the military sentiment that pervaded German society, as became plain when the army overstepped the mark in their treatment of the citizens of Zabern in Alsace in 1913. The army, having further antagonised the local civilians took various illegal actions to punish civilians for such 'crimes' as laughing at the soldiers. The Social Democrats managed to draw together a large majority in the Reichstag for a resolution critical of the army's conduct. The coalition quickly dissolved however, when the Kaiser made some small concessions and the government raised the fear of democratic control of the army. The officer chiefly responsible for the abuses was acquitted by a court-martial. Too vigorous an opposition to militarism raised the prospect of a military *coup d'etat* in the supposed interest of Germany's future in a threatened world. In Germany, as in France, the military longed to deal with the 'traitors to the nation', the Socialists. But in Germany it could be more than mere talk. In 1914 Rosa Luxemburg, a leading left-wing Socialist, was sentenced to a year's imprisonment on a charge of having urged workers not to obey any call to fight against France. Pending appeal, she was again prosecuted for criticising the army. At the outbreak of war, Bethmann-Hollweg had difficulty in dissuading some of the Generals from arresting the leading Socialists. When reflecting, about that time, on the steps that had brought Germany to the eve of war, Bethmann blamed the aimlessness of German policies but also 'the national parties which with their racket about foreign policy want to preserve and strengthen their party position.'

The complete readiness of the German government to support Austria-Hungary in 1914, so important an element in the outbreak of war, arose from internal as well as external needs. The break-up of the Austro-Hungarian empire had to be avoided not only because it was Germany's only reliable ally but also because such an event would bring into the German empire sufficient Austrian Germans to threaten Prussian predominance. Having fought already to secure their leadership in the Empire, the Prussian ruling elite had no desire to sacrifice it. There was much speculation in Vienna on the comparative advantages and disadvantages to the Austro-Hungarian Empire of a war. In mid-1914 it was chiefly the Hungarian leaders who retained grave doubts of the value of acquiring more Slav subjects in a Balkan war; the Magyar ruling class were already very much of a minority. Still, 'in Vienna,' writes Norman Stone, 'the grotesque notion gained ground that all nationalism would be destroyed in the suppression of its most obvious manifestation . . . Serbia was, despite itself, a symbol of the monarchy's ills'. Zeman, another historian, comments: 'Having abandoned hope of solving the South Slav question peacefully the rulers of the monarchy delivered the future of the state into the hands of the soldiers.'

With hind-sight we might say that Russia had compelling reasons for avoiding war. How could the Imperial rulers, with recent experience of war producing revolution, with a grievous problem of national minorities and the prospect of their siding with an enemy, with grave industrial unrest and internal disorder, consider the possibility of war? To some prominent figures war was unthinkable. Witte, the former Prime Minister, thought Russia could not fight a major war and secretly let the Germans know as much. But for many, war was seen as a unifying force and certainly preferable to international humiliation such as followed the Balkan wars of 1912-13. Rodzyanko, President of the Fourth Duma, urged 'The Straits must become ours. A war will be joyfully welcomed and will raise the government's prestige.' That was a representative view for the Octobrist party, which represented by no means the most conservative elements in Russian society. They were chiefly landowners with much to lose in revolution and rural unrest and their expansionism may be seen as an attempt to distract the people by spectacular foreign success.

The influence of the Duma and its parties was considerable but constitutionally the ultimate decisions in foreign policy and defence belonged with the Tsar. Even so, he chafed at the small restrictions that the Duma's position placed on his absolute power. He was not the stuff of which constitutional monarchs are made: even on the eve of the 1917 revolution, when the British Ambassador urged him to make concessions, he replied 'Do you mean that *I* am to regain the confidence of my people or that they are to regain *mine.*' He ignored the constitution in 1907,dissolving the Duma and altering the electoral law. He proposed *coup d'etat* to various ministers in 1909, 1910 and 1913. In June 1914 he suggested to ministers that the Duma simply be consulted on proposed laws and that the majority opinion be ignored if unacceptable. His ministers were well aware of the dangers presented by the unrest amongst workers that erupted in the same month. After the assassination of the Austrian Archduke at Sarajevo and the ultimatum to Serbia, a Russian acceptance of Austrian annexations in the Balkans would have compounded the government's unpopularity. A war, however, although a great risk, offered the Tsar and his ministers the chance of re-uniting his people. And so it emerged, the Duma voted funds for war with a surge of patriotism and the people on the day war was declared massed in the square outside the Winter Palace. It was here in 1905 that a petitioning crowd had been fired on and from thence revolution had spread, but now they cheered and sang 'God Save the Tsar'. Denied his hopes of *coup d'etat,* the Tsar now had his powers extended under the emergency war-time conditions. As Sazanov, the Foreign Minister, afterwards remarked, the mobilisation 'was unavoidable for internal political reasons.'

5. DIPLOMATIC AND MILITARY RIVALRIES 1909-14

THE AFTERMATH OF THE BOSNIAN ANNEXATION

The Serbian Foreign Minister Ninčič noted, many years after the war, 'The grave events which preceded the declaration of war on Serbia in 1914 all developed within the framework of the [Bosnian annexation of 1908-9].' Certainly the annexation was not the end of the affair. Aehrenthal, the Austrian Foreign Minister, anticipated the complete extermination of the Serbian 'revolutionaries'. In Serbia the secret plotting that culminated in the assassination at Sarajevo was given a new impetus. In many other ways, too, 1909 provided the elements that made war possible. A condition of the Austro-Hungarian success had been the promise of German military support in the event of Russia reacting to a Balkan advance by Austria. Since the Schlieffen plan dictated an advance against France prior to throwing full weight against Russia, the mechanism by which a Balkan conflict would escalate into a general war was ready for operation. Further, since nations seldom bear their humiliations gracefully, the Russian government interpreted their diplomatic reverse as an invitation to ensure, by renewed military preparations, that it did not recur. Finally, 1909 provides a bench mark for the Anglo-German naval rivalry. The exaggerated reaction of the British public, although not spontaneous, was heightened by German reluctance to be conciliatory over the Balkans. This reluctance to compromise, as seen from the British side, seemed particularly marked in naval affairs. The Kaiser in late 1908 was interviewed for the London *Daily Telegraph.* He attempted to paint a picture of himself as a true friend of Britain in the face of the hostility of the German people. It was a ham-handed affair creating some concern and some wonder in Britain, but causing a major stir in Germany where its diplomatic *gaucherie* was felt deeply. Bülow received some part of the criticism and his failure to defend the Kaiser with the vigour desired by the court left a marked resentment. That was increased by Bülow's contemplating some lessening in the rate of naval building in order to secure in exchange some diplomatic advantage from Britain. He had in mind British neutrality in an Anglo-French war, but the eyes of Tirpitz were fixed more simply on a reduction in the British rate of warship construction. Tirpitz, with the support of the Kaiser, was able to impose conditions on the negotiations which pre-ordained them to failure, for the British government was concerned for a meaningful reduction in the naval race. Bülow resigned in July 1909 but Bethmann-Hollweg, his successor, was no more successful in slowing the arms race.

THE MOROCCAN CRISIS

It was not, however, in the east that the European crisis came, but in the west. The agreement reached at the Algeciras conference of 1906, while allowing French predominance in Morocco to continue, had also protected the rights of other powers and thus left ample room for international tension. In 1908 the arrest of three German deserters from the French Foreign Legion while they were under the protection of the German consul brought forth much strong talk in the French newspapers and it is significant that, although the issue was resolved peacefully, the German government contemplated sending a warship to assert its rights. It was plain in France that Morocco was now an issue involving national honour. An attempt was made to take the heat out of this extra-European conflict of interests through the negotiation of an agreement between the two countries in 1909 that France had a special responsibility for the maintenance of law and order. Arab feelings of resentment at these European intrusions arose, exacerbated by the failure of the Sultan to resist. Tribes to the south of Fez, alarmed at French expansion, rose in revolt. They proclaimed a new Sultan and advanced on Fez and the reigning Sultan.

There were various ways of reacting to the Moroccan situation. The one chosen was partly a product of pressure-group tactics within France. Etienne, the chief Moroccan enthusiast in the Chamber of Deputies and leader of the Colonial party, influenced the few ministers who were still in Paris during Easter 1911. The Foreign Minister, Cruppi, was, as all observers agreed, inexperienced and too easily lead, the War Minister was anxious for Etienne's support in a bid he was soon proposing to make for the Presidency. The result was that French troops were despatched to support the Sultan's government and incidentally strengthen the French position. It looked very much like a characteristic colonial conquest, for the French troops attacked Fez, the Moorish capital. There was no immediate opposition from the German government and Cruppi showed, in the opinion of Isvolsky, the former Russian Foreign Minister and now Ambassador to Paris, 'a dangerous and insufficiently grounded optimism.' Izvolsky saw that Germany had reserved the right to complain of any infringement of the Algeciras Act and was simply waiting to choose the right moment to bring the matter to a head. The Spanish government, which had traditional interests in the area, protested in May at the French action. On July 1, 1911 the German gun-boat *Panther* anchored at the port of Agadir. Negotiations for a Franco-German settlement of the issue had begun before this and there was talk already of giving Germany part of the Congo as the price of her acquiescence in this French occupation of Fez. Kiderlin, the German Foreign Secretary, decided to send the gun-boat to strengthen the German hand in negotiation, believing that a strong line would ensure success. The dramatic gesture created a greater reaction in London than in Paris. In the latter capital, a new French ministry had entered office only the day before 'Agadir' and Caillaux, the Premier, was reluctant to take resistance to Germany to the point of war. Even when Kiderlin put forward his demand for the whole of the Congo, Caillaux, armed with sceptical reports on its value, decided about July 17 or 18 to offer Germany a considerable section of the Congo. Caillaux kept the negotiations in his own hands to some extent since the permanent officials at the French Foreign Ministry took, in keeping with some sections of the press, a more belligerent attitude.

Although the Agadir crisis started as a Franco-German skirmish comparable with others that had gone before, it took on the character of an Anglo-German confrontation of major importance. Until the arrival of the *Panther*, the British Foreign Office had principally been concerned that France and Germany would reach some Moroccan agreement without Britain being fully consulted. British interests there – keeping Morocco open to British trade and not threatening the Royal Navy's position in the Mediterranean – might be ignored, but more important the Entente might be weakened if the French became accustomed to settling their differences directly with Germany. The arrival of the *Panther* had a number of unfortunate effects: it caused uncertainty in Britain because the German demands were not clear, it made still greater the prospect of a Franco-German settlement of the question, a settlement which would, by humiliating France, weaken the Entente. It seemed to be the first Moroccan crisis all over again. The French government was to have the lesson driven home that the Entente was useless to protect it in a direct negotiation with Germany. The Entente policy was strongly supported by the British Foreign Office which read the situation almost entirely in terms of maintenance of the Entente against this threat. When the news arrived of the German demand for the Congo, one official wrote 'This is a trial of strength if it is anything. Concession . . . means defeat with all its inevitable consequences'. Sir Edward Grey was very much in tune with this attitude and his first reaction was to send a Royal Naval vessel to Morocco.

The British Cabinet, however, intervened to prevent the despatch of a warship and while agreeing that the German government could not settle the question without consulting Britain, believed that the French, too, must expect to make concessions, perhaps even in Morocco itself. Such a decision may seem a major reverse for the course of action urged by Grey and particularly by his official advisers, but it was rather part of the continuing tug-of-war for the control of British foreign policy with the Radicals among the government's members, both inside and outside the Cabinet, enjoying a temporary success. How temporary it was became obvious on July 21 when Lloyd George, a man of unequivocally Radical background who was prone to refer to the War Minister as Minister for Slaughter, made a major intervention. As Chancellor of the Exchequer he was chosen to give the major annual speech to the financial interests of the City of London at the Mansion House. In the course of it, he said:

> [If] peace could only be preserved . . . by allowing Britain to be treated where her interests were vitally affected as if she were of no account in the Cabinet of nations, then I say emphatically that peace at that price would be a humiliation intolerable for a great country like ours to endure.

This talk of honour and dignity had its familiar effect of raising the heat and lowering the light in the international discourse. The speech was directed chiefly at Germany but her offence was the exclusion of Britain from the negotiations. Although it gave support to France and the Entente it also bore interpretation as a warning that the French government should not engage in negotiations without full consultation with London. Caillaux's decision in Paris to negotiate on the basis of an offer of part of the Congo had already been taken, so the tone and manner of the intervention was perhaps unnecessarily strong. The historian Gerhard Ritter, a student at the time, recalls 'the wave of fear that swept the German people.' The day before the speech the British and French General Staffs had concerted plans for the outbreak of war and the Admiralty issued orders for the concentration of the Atlantic fleet at Portsmouth. The newspapers in Britain and Germany swelled out with a great deal of patriotic writing and the constant thought that Germany might enforce her demands by military means heightened the pitch of the British reaction.

When the Entente partners looked at their practical readiness for war, the story was rather different. Internally, the Caillaux ministry was scarcely in the saddle and Britain was in the midst of serious industrial unrest. When the secretary of the railwaymen's union wrote on August 18, 'War has begun' he referred to the class war launched by the general strike on the railways and Lloyd George had to invoke the international dangers to resolve the conflict. Moreover, the Russian government had little concern for supporting her ally in a conflict so remote from her interests. Nor could the Entente powers count on the smooth operation of the military machine. The armed forces therefore built on their earlier peacetime co-operation: the general staffs concerting their military efforts more closely and the navies, following earlier talks, agreed in August to share control of the Mediterranean, the French to watch the west end and deal with the Austrian and Italian naval threat, while the Royal Navy watched the eastern Mediterranean. Thus far had the traditional predominance of Britain in the Mediterranean been forsaken in the interests of concentration in the North Sea. The possibility of the French Navy controlling the Straits of Dover, from Dover, had even been discussed. The degree of co-ordination between the forces of the two nations, much of it very limited and verbal rather than written, still greatly exceeded that of the two arms of the defences of Britain. A meeting of the Committee of Imperial Defence was held in August and revealed even more clearly a truth of long standing – the army and navy could not resolve their differences in planning. The navy could not offer the safe transport across the channel of the four divisions of troops that the army was resolved to send in the event of war. The Admiralty made the less impressive showing at the meeting and the Prime Minister, Asquith, resolved to make it accept the War Office plan for war. 'The present position,' he commented 'in which everything is locked up in the brain of a single taciturn Admiral is both ridiculous and dangerous.' Winston Churchill took over the Admiralty and joined the inner group of ministers who managed the crisis during the hot summer. Lloyd George and Churchill, Britain's two great twentieth century war leaders, now had their baptism of war-like preparations and showed every sign of having enjoyed it.

In Paris the negotiations continued, producing crises with each deadlock. There were plainly two aspects to the bargain: how much of the Congo was Germany to be given and to what extent would France be allowed a free hand in Morocco. In September the German government proposed joint economic exploitation of Morocco and joint rule in some areas. Having aroused the enthusiasm of companies with interests in southern Morocco, such as the Hamburg-Marokko Gesellschaft, they found it difficult to ignore the supposed potential of the area. Acceptance would have been a humiliating reduction of the French designs for Morocco and would have renewed the exclusion of Britain from the settlement. The contestants made ready for the war they thought near and the Belgian army started to mobilise. Again, a compromise was reached which recognised the French right to occupy parts of the country at the invitation of the Sultan and also the right of the French government to represent the Sultan in foreign affairs and control his finances. In equatorial Africa the chief provision was the surrender to Germany of part of the French Congo. An occasion for occupation of Morocco was very quickly found and it became a French protectorate, that is, little short of a colony, in March 1912.

THE RESULTS OF THE MOROCCAN CRISIS

The results of the Agadir incident were uniformly bad. The settlement was reached at the price of the Congolese and Moroccans who were brought under clear colonial domination. Nor can it be said that the settlement was welcomed in Europe. Even in France, after an initially favourable newspaper reaction, enthusiasm for it declined with the publication of the Franco-Spanish agreement of 1904 which had recognised a sphere of influence for Spain in northern Morocco. The outburst of nationalism which accompanied the incident helped fire the 'National Revival' in France. In Germany, public opinion had not fully grasped the significance of Agadir as a bargaining counter for the securing of territory elsewhere and saw only surrender in Morocco. Moltke and others of the generals and officials, saw the incident as a chance for a successful war lost and criticised the Kaiser for his apparent lack of nerve. At first Austria had played to Germany the same role as Russia to France, expressing a lack of concern. Indeed, as one prominent statesman in the Dual Monarchy remarked, the trouble about Germany as an ally was that she was always in hot water.

The result of the Agadir crisis in Britain in some respects resembles the result on the continent. There was the same stimulus to military preparations. Without Agadir, recalled the Secretary of the Committee of Imperial Defence, it would have been impossible to undertake the measures preparatory for war: the appointment of a new First Lord of the Admiralty, the agreement on continental intervention if circumstances demanded, further concentration of the Royal Navy in home waters. More interesting was the strong Radical reaction in Britain against war and against an aggressive foreign policy. The full Cabinet heard for the first time of the Anglo-French military conversations which had started more than five years before and government Members of Parliament launched a vigorous drive to secure closer control of foreign policy by thc formation of a Liberal Foreign Affairs Committee. Outside the walls of the House of Commons, the liberal public also became restive. One contemporary periodical, critical of Grey, wrote: 'Peace is always his object, but peace in the panoply of war, peace that goes to the razor-edge of strife . . . for a non-British interest . . . [He] has changed the whole face of foreign policy to one of entangling alliances.' ('The British Radicals and the Balance of

Power, 1902-1914', H.S. Weinroth, *Historical Journal,* XIII (4), p.677.) From this reassertion of opinion there came a number of Cabinet decisions designed to lessen the risk of war. There were to be no new military conversations engaged in without cabinet approval and the continuing consultations would not be regarded as committing the British government to war. That was only a limited victory for the radicals, for the two armies continued to concert their efforts. Nor was the attempt to lessen the Anglo-German naval rivalry more successful. The navy was the main instrument of British defence and the construction rate could not, it was thought, be too drastically pruned. Lord Haldane was sent to Berlin to negotiate some understanding in February 1912. That was a genuine attempt to secure agreement but there were those on both sides (and in France) who regarded such an object as neither possible nor desirable. The failure of this mission is one clear indication of the inflexibility of the positions adopted by the two sides and is a measure, too, of the militarism of the times. Another indication of the difficulties of radical attempts to control foreign policy is provided by the exchange of letters in November 1912 between Grey and the French Ambassador who had requested them. Although they made clear the limitations of the military consultations which 'ought not to be regarded as an engagement that commits either government to action', they formally recognised the consultations and provided that the two governments should concert their plans in time of crisis.

THE BALKAN WARS

The French dispatch of troops to Fez and the subsequent German attempt to secure colonial compensation set off a chain reaction. The Italian government delivered an ultimatum to the Ottoman Empire, claiming Tripoli. This action was on the basis of an agreement of 1900 by which Italy's right to extend its influence in Tripoli was recognised by France in the event of a French alteration to the political and territorial status of Morocco. Such an assault on the Turkish government was sure to weaken the rule of the Young Turks, those reforming pro-German elements that had taken power in Constantinople in 1908. In that way the Moroccan crisis had links with the Balkans, for the nations and embryo-nations there saw the chance of shaking off the Turkish yoke or extending their territory and influence. In other ways, too, there were links. The Russian government, its eyes ever fixed on the Straits, claimed French support for an attempt to secure control there, when the time came to make it, in exchange for the support Russia had given over Morocco. She had already gained such an understanding from Italy and this would have helped clear her path further. The French government were reluctant to commit themselves explicitly although they did make sympathetic sounds.

The Tripolitan war was, remarked the Bulgarian Minister of Finance, a heaven-sent opportunity to weaken the two main opponents of Slavdom. Here was a chance to shake off the claims of Ottoman and Austrian influence in the Balkans and enlarge each of the States to reach those boundaries regarded, on the basis of language or geography or economics or other factors, as being natural. Large ambitions are not confined to great powers; a golden opportunity such as this brought the Balkan nations together in a League. Russian representatives in Bulgaria and Serbia smoothed its path, but the military convention that bound the two together detailing the division of function in the war effort was their own. So, too, was the military understanding between Greece and Bulgaria. Tiny Montenegro joined late in the piece and by early October 1912 the Balkan Alliance was complete. The Kaiser, with a characteristic flash of misjudgment, saw the alliance as the nucleus of a seventh great power. It was in reality a temporary structure held together only by fear of its opponents and hope of mutual territorial gain. An insurrection in Albania against Turkish rule was in progress in the summer of 1912 and could provide the flash-point for war.

The Great Powers viewed these development in the Balkans without enthusiasm. As patrons of these small states they knew themselves to be strong enough to influence them but not strong enough to direct them. By facilitating or obstructing loans or by conferring or withholding trading advantages they could exert pressure, but too great a pressure could be counter-productive. If the Russian government, for example, tried too obviously to restrain Serbian demands it would lay itself open to the charge of being unsympathetic to pan-Slav feeling. If the Austro-Hungarian government pressed the King of Bulgaria too strongly to make territorial concessions to Rumania (which was linked by alliance to the Central Powers) then he might look to Russia for support. This knowledge that the Balkan nations were not passive instruments of the Great Powers but were volatile elements that might lead the powers into war, encouraged caution. The allies of the two powers most closely interested, Russia and Austria-Hungary, showed little inclination at first to urge them on and those two powers saw the problems of exploiting the situation effectively, for it was difficult to support one nation without offending the others. The powers, under the guidance of the British government, came out strongly for the preservation of the existing state of affairs. The decision was not arrived at purely on the negative lines suggested: a positive desire to support the Ottoman empire played a big part in influencing Britain and France.

The plans of the diplomats, the somewhat musty reincarnation of the concert of Europe, were exploded in the first few weeks of the war. The widespread expectation that the fortunes of war would favour the Turks was proved incorrect. War was declared by Montenegro on the day after the powers published their declaration insisting on the *status quo.* The other states joined in, the Bulgarians driving towards Constaninople with such success that by early November the Turkish defences had fallen back to the Chatalja line, the fighting could be heard from the capital and the King of Bulgaria was preparing his uniforms for entry into the ancient city which commanded the Straits. The Serbs, despite the absence of the Bulgarian support, promised under the convention, advanced into Macedonia. This Ottoman province was an object of attraction to Serbs, Bulgarians and Greeks and such was the ethnic diversity of the area that all could produce some justification. The 1912 census broke the one and a quarter million population into approximately 40% Moslem 40% Greek 10% Bulgarian as the main groups. The pearl of the area was Salonika, occupied by the Greeks on 9 November and the Bulgarians on the following day. The Austro-Hungarian government, watching these developments with dismay, suggested that land-locked Serbia might find its outlet to the sea at Salonika, but the Serbs refused to pursue this transparent device to embroil the three allies. Instead, the Serbian forces drove west reaching the Adriatic in Mid-November. The Montenegrins also had an interest here for their ambitions were directed south and they laid siege to Scutari. If Montenegro secured Scutari they could offer their allies, Serbia, access to the coast and the only thing worse than that, from an Austrian point of view, was if Serbia was itself to secure an Adriatic port, say Durazzo. The idea behind the 'Pig War' had been to ensure Serbian economic dependence of Austria-Hungary. A port would allow her to break free from this form of bondage. It would constitute not only a financial reverse to the Dual Monarchy but also a political one, for a prosperous and enlarged Serbia would act as a magnet for Slavs within Hungary particularly. Such a development was all the more dangerous, for Serbian and Montenegrin troops had occupied the Sanjak (or administrative area) of Novi Pazar, an area some thirty to sixty miles wide separating Serbia from Montenegro. The Sanjak was important to Austria-Hungary as a wedge to keep these two Slav nations apart and as having military significance, providing a direct entry into the disputed areas of Macedonia leading down to Salonika, which the Austrians had long wished to unite to themselves by railway. Because of its importance it had been garrisoned by Austrian troops to 1909 but Aehrenthal had surrendered that and it now fell into Slav hands.

These then were the key regions: Adrianople and the approaches to

Constantinople, central Macedonia and the Vardar valley which lead to Salonika, the Adriatic coast of Albania with Scutari and the Sanjak. Lastly, there might be added Silistria, a rounding out of the Rumanian possessions which passed, with the effect on Rumanian opinion of the Bulgarian territorial success, from the state of being 'desirable', through 'necessary', to becoming 'an inadequate starting point'.

This first Balkan war posed great difficulties for the Triple Alliance. It was due for renewal, and the negotiations with Italy continued during the war, giving it bargaining power just as later negotiations for the linking of Rumania with the Central Powers also gave it leverage. It was difficult for Austria to pursue the policy of supporting an enlarged Bulgaria (as a counterweight to Serbia) without offending Rumania. Even the very heart of the alliance, Austro-German relations, was in a poor state. A promise had been made to the Tsar in 1910 at Potsdam that Germany would not support Austrian aggression in the Balkans. Then, at Agadir, further strain had been put on the alliance by the lack of Austrian support for Germany. Finally, the Balkans were not viewed in the same light by the two powers. The Austrian commercial link, indeed her wish for economic domination there, was recognised, but German trade expansion was in the Ottoman empire rather than the Balkan nations. For all these reasons it was difficult for Austria-Hungary to intervene decisively. Although there was no shortage of pressure on Berchtold (who became Austrian Foreign Minister in 1912) from army and other sources he refused to launch an attack on Serbia and even reconciled himself to the loss of the Sanjak. He recognised that, 'We ourselves are responsible not only for the formation of the Balkan alliance but also for the distrust with which we are regarded by all the chancellories of Europe and this has created a unity of action among them which would not otherwise exist.' Kiderlin, the German Foreign Secretary, was no supporter of the Bülow policy of involvement in the Balkans and worked for co-operation with the British government to prevent the conflict spreading throughout Europe.

The situation was little better for the Entente powers. Although Hartwig, the Russian representative in Serbia, gave an exaggerated view of the degree of support the Serbs might expect, the developments caused most members of the Russian government concern rather than delight. The advance of the Bulgarian army towards Constantinople in late 1912 caused Sazanov to consider seriously the need for Russian intervention to ensure that if the Straits were to fall to anybody, it must be to Russia. By late November the Austrian army had partially mobilised in Galicia and on the Serbian frontier, and Russia also conducted a partial mobilisation of its southern commands. The Russian government could not, at least, claim that its ally was restraining it; Poincaré worked closely with Izvolsky, the

Russian Ambassador. French public opinion welcomed the success of the Balkan League as a reverse for the Central Powers and a victory for French arms and finance, both of which had been amply supplied to the Balkan states. Working from that basis, Izvolsky and Poincaré started to prepare the ground for a war that would come from the Balkans. A good deal of Russian money was distributed to the French newspapers to influence them to favour Poincare's external, and internal, policies; it was desirable for the sake of the alliance that its opponents among the Radicals and Socialists should be kept out of office. Poincaré was influenced by military advice on the suitability of the time for war and he saw the need to strengthen the Russian military effort by showing an interest in the Balkans. Although the evidence is not entirely satisfactory, it does seem that he enlarged the Franco-Russian alliance in two respects. First, he recognised that the French government had an interest in the Balkans to maintain the European balance of power and secondly, in discussing the possibility of Austrian intervention in the Balkans, he said 'Broadly, it all comes to this: if Russia goes into the war, France will do the same as we know that in this matter Germany would stand at Austria's back.' Just as, in 1909, the German government had effectively enlarged the terms of its alliance with the Austrian-Hungarian government, so now the French government was moving into the position where a cause of war could come from a Balkan issue and Russia need be no longer the victim of unprovoked aggression, as had been provided by the original convention between the two powers.

The British government was the weak link in the Entente for it still tended to cling to its traditional policy of supporting the Ottoman Empire. Such a position made co-operation with the German government easier and the two worked together to resolve the crisis. Indeed, one of the major differences between the Balkan crises of 1912-13 and that of 1914 was in the willingness of the two powers to co-ordinate their efforts. They agreed in October 1912 to engage in negotiations (to be kept secret from their allies) and to adhere to any agreement reached in the face of opposition from the other powers. When the fighting stalemated and the Balkan powers made an armistice in December, this agreement bore fruit in the Ambassadors' Conference convened by Grey at London. The main sticking point, the Serbian access to the sea, was resolved by the creation of an independent Albania with, however, Serbia to have access to a port for her commerce via an internationally supervised railway line.

The hopes of the London conference were temporarily interrupted at the end of January when, as a result of a change of Turkish government, hostilities were resumed. In March and April, the dangers of an armed Austrian intervention again rose high, for the Montenegrans, with Serbian support, continued the seige of Scutari. Joint intervention by the powers was not at first sufficient to deter Serbia and the situation was made worse when the Turkish commander was induced by bribery to surrender Scutari. The desirability of war was discussed at the Austro-Hungarian Crown Council of 2 May and, as was to happen in 1914, the Hungarian influence was against the war. The fear of financial difficulties and the alienation of Italy made the government wait yet again, but the threat of war that was in the air and the clear German support that emerged led to united international pressure on Montenegro. Miniscule Montenegro had, by confronting Austria-Hungary and threatening her policy of keeping Serbia land-bound through the creation of a united Albania, brought Europe to the verge of war. Not all were distressed. King Nicholas of Montenegro is said to have bought Austrian government bonds when their price was low through danger of war and resold them with the arrival of peace.

THE SECOND BALKAN WAR JUNE 1913

The peace settlement reached on 30 May had in it the seeds of its own destruction. Bulgaria had done well for itself but Serbia had, partly because deprived of promised Bulgarian military support, failed to secure the parts of Macedonia which interested it, the Vardar valley and access to Salonika. So, it allied with Greece to wrest these areas from Bulgaria. The Greeks had their own differences with the Bulgarians, for the treaty had not settled the possession of Salonika and Kavala, another important port on the Aegean. Bulgaria was thus surrounded by those aggrieved at its much enlarged territory, for Rumania, having stayed out of the war at the request of the Central Powers, saw now the chance of securing the rewards of such forebearance. Nor was the Ottoman empire prepared to accept easily the loss of Adrianople. Bulgaria launched, undeclared, the second Balkan war by attacking the Serbs and Greeks at the end of June. Here, surely, was the triumph of Austro-Hungarian policy, for the Balkan alliance was in disarray and there was the chance of restructuring the Balkans to better contain Serbia. Berchtold, the Foreign Minister, wished Austria to fight on the side of Bulgaria so as the better to reduce Serbian power but this policy was ruled out for two reasons: first, and most important, neither Germany nor Italy would support it, and secondly, it remained difficult to reconcile a pro-Bulgarian and pro-Rumanian policy. If part of Bulgaria was to be given to the Rumanians, and Silistria was no longer sufficient for Rumanian opinion, then Bulgaria would have to be given compensation and the obvious candidate was the port of Kavala opposite the island of Thatos which was to be Bulgarian, but this in turn would antagonise the Greeks who were seen, in Berlin at least, as likely supporters of the central powers; a belief the Kaiser reached more easily because his sister was Queen of Greece.

After major reverses in the field, the settlement was, like the war, quickly concluded. The Balkan powers met at Bucharest and the peace was signed in August before the great powers had time to intervene. Germany, impatient of Austria-Hungary's concern with small Balkan towns – William II treated Vienna as 'completely cracked' – recognised the treaty as final and the two most interested parties, Austria and Russia, were, as it turned out, left without allies to support any attempt at revision. The Balkan nations had very largely worked out their own fate but in doing so inescapably affected the relations of those two Great Powers, so the results are best looked at, initially at least, through their eyes.

RESULTS OF THE BALKAN WARS

Austria-Hungary could draw little comfort from the Balkan wars and their aftermath. The Balkan League which might have left it completely surrounded by enemies, save for Germany to the north, had, it is true, split up, but there were to appear signs of its being reassembled. Some statesmen in Vienna considered that the Entente powers were attempting that and the suspicion, true or not, was an influence which must be taken into account. The wars were no victory for the Central Powers: the Ottoman Empire, a likely ally, had been almost thrust out of the peninsula, Serbia was greatly enlarged in area and correspondingly more buoyant in spirit and attractive to the Dual Monarchy's own Slav population. The situation was worsened by the possibility of a union of Serbia and Montenegro, as contemplated by the two kings. They now shared a border, having conquered the Sanjak of Novipazar together, and union would have cut away the root of Austro-Hungarian policy in the Balkans by creating the nucleus of a 'Yugoslavia' and giving Serbia access to the Adriatic. On top of this, there remained the difficulty of balancing the conflicting claims of Bulgaria and Rumania. Bulgaria waited for the opportunity to redress the 'wrongs' done in the second Balkan war and looked to the Dual Monarchy for help, but any suggestion that the peace of Bucharest should be altered alarmed the Rumanians. Rumania's central importance derived partly from her military position; if she threw in her lot with the Central Powers she could provide five army corps on the right flank for an invasion of Russia and correspondingly lighten the burden on the Central Powers, which could foresee other calls on their troops in a major conflict. If she fought with Russia, the Tsarist forces would have direct access to the central Balkans and the possibility of raiding Hungary over the undefended paths through the Carpathians. Its relation with the Dual Monarchy was particularly sensitive because of the Rumanian concern for the welfare of

The Balkans in 1913

kinsmen suffering under Magyar domination in Hungary. Although bound to the Central Powers by alliance, popular feeling was so strong against the very thought of fighting alongside Austro-Hungarian troops, that the king refused to tell his foreign minister of the existence of the treaty.

The wars had made painfully obvious the gaps between the Balkan policies of Berlin and Vienna. Their end produced a swing in German policy towards fuller support for Austria-Hungary. In October 1913, when Serbia showed reluctance to withdraw her troops behind the Albanian border lines agreed on at the London Ambassadors' conference, the Austro-Hungarian government issued a generally worded but quite clear threat. Berchtold had resisted a great many previous suggestions along these lines. Even the Hungarian Prime Minister, Tisza, supported firmness on this occasion, perhaps because of the way in which Conrad, the Chief of Staff, posed the problem: either the Serbs must be incorporated in the Monarchy or else made subordinate by a show of force. As far as Magyar domination was concerned perhaps the latter was the lesser of the two evils. Still more significant was the return of the German government to full support for its ally. William II was aware that his policy of winning Rumania and Greece had temporarily offended the Monarchy. Now, however, the Kaiser was prepared with his hand on the hilt to speak of his readiness 'to draw the sword' in support and he suggested a crucial reason why: If it came to 'a serious armed conflict . . . we Germans stand with you and behind you: but we can in no case be indifferent as to whether the twenty divisions of your army are tied up for operations against the South Slav or not.'

WAR READINESS

This calculation of the international scene in terms of numbers of effective troops likely to be available in war was characteristic of these years. The German army bill of 1913 was partly justified by the need for making good the reduction in support by Austria-Hungary because of her Balkan involvements. It provided for 117,000 more men and 19,000 more commissioned and non-commissioned officers. Its roots went back to the Agadir incident and beyond, in the contemplation of the gap between the military strength of the likely contestants in the next war. The Russian mobilisation during the Balkan wars played its part: the War Minister announced in the same month 'that Germany could not allow Russia to mobilise again and should this in fact happen he would call up the reserve'. Internal political considerations played their part as well: there could not be a large army bill in 1912 because the navy was given precedence, but the delay built up the pressure on the government for a major increase. The Army League formed in 1912 had recruited almost 300,000 members after one year, the Pan-German League pressed hard for an increase and Colonel Ludendorff, a staff officer later to be prominent on the western front, kept the Chief of Staff, Moltke, up to the mark. The increase, triggering off enlargements in the Entente armies, did little to brighten Moltke's gloomy assessment of the German position by 1914.

The Balkan wars provided the Entente powers with little consolation. Izvolsky, looking from the Russian viewpoint, saw that the wars had saved St Petersburg the difficulty of having to play umpire in the clashing Balkan claims in Macedonia. It allowed the Russian government also to extract full value from pan-Slav feeling; early 1914 saw a parade of Balkan dignitaries to Russia. Ritual expressions of mutual support and sympathy were made; these were tempered by a good deal of cynicism on both sides but the Central Powers could not but be concerned at the sight of Păsić, the Serbian premier, or the Rumanian Crown Prince exchanging pleasantries in St Petersburg. There was, however, one obvious area in which Russian policy had failed. Yet again, Russia had not secured control of the Straits. Indeed, this long-pursued goal seemed more remote than ever when in early November it became plain that the German General, Liman von Sanders was to command the Turkish troops at Constantinople. Holding other offices, and with the support of other German specialists seconded to train the Turkish army, Sanders had virtual control of the Straits. A compromise was finally reached whereby Sanders, while keeping his other positions, ceased to have control at Constantinople, but not before the Russian government had considered various measures to secure its end, including the seizure of the Turkish town of Bayazid as hostage for a satisfactory settlement. The records of the Russian ministerial meetings which discussed this make interesting reading. There was a marked reluctance to act without concerting with the Entente partners and general agreement that it was essential to avoid steps that might lead to war with Germany. A closer examination of the possibility of action against Turkey revealed the weakened state of the Russian forces. In answer to other increases the Russian army was enlarged. But the realities became plain when the serving officers and ministers examined the possibility of seizing the Straits. This would, it was agreed, involve a general European war.

> According to the war plans drawn up to meet the eventuality of a battle on the western front, all the troops from the inland commands must be brought up to join the troops operating on the western front; it would therefore unfortunately be impossible to find troops from the inland commands in the Empire to send to this front to replace the southern army corps proposed to be used in the landing operation, in order to make it possible to send this army corps to Constantinople whatever the circumstances. The Foreign Minister asked whether the situation would be altered by the increase in our army now in progress; the Chief of General Staff replied this increase would consist only of the formation of two army corps in 1915 and 1916. These army corps will be stationed on our western frontier and serve only to balance the recent increases in the German and Austrian armies. (F. Stieve, *Izvolsky and the First World War,* 1926, p.233, Minutes of Conference of 8 Feb. 1914.)

The difficulty of providing troops for the plan was added to by weaknesses in war material, communications and mobilisation. The gap between the capacity of the Russian army and its self-confidence was becoming very evident.

The strength and disposition of the Russian army was a matter of intimate concern to the French government. If Russian forces could mobilise quickly and launch a major offensive on Germany's eastern front, German forces, intended for the invasion of France, would have to be diverted. Poincaré devoted himself particularly to this task, visiting St Petersburg in August 1912 and sending, as Ambassador to Russia, Delcassé, with the task of negotiating closer military understanding. The French had, so they thought, played their part in strengthening the Entente forces by the enactment of the three-year military law. That was passed in August 1913 and was, as we have seen, greatly influenced by home politics. Its full effect in producing a larger and better trained army would be some years in being felt. The effective strength of the Russian army also being increased, although again the increase would take time to have effect, Delcassé had to work at the problem of construction of strategic railway lines to the western front so as to speed up the transfer of Russian troops there. As an inducement the French government offered to allow Russian railways loans of up to 500 million francs to be raised in Paris annually for five years and that was agreed in December 1913, too late, however, to aid the war effort although perhaps not too late to influence the decision for war.

ANGLO-GERMAN CO-OPERATION

Bethmann, the German chancellor, writing shortly before the assassination at Sarajevo, recognised that Russia might be expected to take a stronger line in the next Balkan crisis. 'Whether it will come to a European conflagration will depend entirely on the attitude of Germany and England.' What prospect was there of Anglo-German co-operation? It is a question well worth asking, for one of the disadvantages of hindsight is that we introduce an element of inevitability not apparent to contemporaries and discard too early growths that seemed to them full of promise. In 1912, before the outbreak of the Balkan wars, discussions had started on 'the interchange of courtesies and territories', as the German representative phrased it. The two protagonists in these talks were Lionel Harcourt, the British Colonial Secretary and his German counterpart, Wilhelm Solf. Harcourt, an admirer of Germany, was one of that large group in the British Cabinet which argued that:

> . . . the assumption that we are in fact members of a new Triple Alliance . . . opposed to the old is so mischievous and dangerous that I think some early opportunity should be taken of making it clear to both France and Russia that any such assumption is wholly opposed to our policy and intention.

He instructed his Permanent Under-Secretary to 'cast your mind over the British Empire – especially Africa and the Pacific – with a view to seeing what we could give and what we want in exchange.' The two governments, finding little that was surplus to requirements in their own territories, tried to reach agreement by exchanging reversionary rights, that is entitlement if the present ruling power either went bankrupt or misruled so flagrantly as to invite dispossession. They looked first at the Congo, for the German ambition was the creation of a broad band of territory across central Africa tapping the trade by railways yet to be built. That however involved offending first the Belgians, and, no matter what the feelings of the African inhabitants of the Congo or their sympathisers, that was impossible. The Belgian government, by allowing German troops transit through their country in time of war, could bring the Anglo-French defensive plans to an end. Second, the French had been given a reversionary right to the Congo when King Leopold first acquired it in 1885. Hence they looked again and successfully negotiated an agreement to divide the rights to the Portuguese colonies in Africa. That was concluded in October 1913 but the details are of little concern for the agreement was not officially recognised by the two governments by August 1914. The German government delayed agreement because they feared that Britain's relations with her oldest ally, Portugal, might prevent full implementation. It is none the less interesting to see just how strongly even so minor an agreement as this was opposed by the British government's own Foreign Office (one official termed Harcourt 'a generous giver of stolen or filched goods') and by the French government which, alarmed at any improvement in Anglo-German relations, threatened to issue a declaration proclaiming the rights of the backward peoples against the politics of force!

The Baghdad railway agreement may be cited as another example of that frail growth, improved Anglo-German relations. It was agreed that the line would terminate at Basra, short of the Persian Gulf where British shipping interests were supreme. British predominance in southern Mesopotamia was recognised, which was important for the defence of India as well as for the oil-fields there (of increasing importance with the Royal Navy's new reliance on oil fuel). In return Germany secured economic advantages elsewhere and the withdrawal of British opposition to the railway.

Against these faltering half-gains must be set a great many signs of the continuing Anglo-German opposition. The most obvious was the naval rivalry. When Churchill introduced his enlarged naval estimates in March 1912 after the failure of the Haldane mission (see page 27), he linked with them a proposal for a naval holiday, a period during which no new vessels would be laid down by either side. The proposal was particularly unwelcome to the German government which could hardly refuse publicly such an offer at a time when it was making heavy demands on the taxpayer for an increased army vote of funds. At all events the offer looked a little thin when re-presented some months later linked with a speeding up in the British programme. Some of Churchill's colleagues showed as little enthusiasm for the proposal as did the German government, and the repeated offers of naval holidays, two from Churchill in 1913 and one from Tirpitz in 1914, were empty gestures. The French government was given constant reassurance from London, and Grey worked against rapprochment, securing the refusal of an invitation from the Emperor for Churchill to attend Kiel week – the German naval 'open day' – in June 1914. Nor was it only a question of whether negotiations continued or not for, as we know, Churchill used every opportunity – speeding up of building, contributions from the colonies, increasing the number of sailors – to increase the effective lead of the Royal Navy.

6. THE JULY CRISIS

AUSTRIA'S BALKAN PROBLEM

Berchtold, the Austrian Foreign Minister, although not a bellicose man, had no desire to preside over the demise of the Dual Monarchy. Yet the signs were not encouraging: the Balkan wars had produced rewards for the enemy Serbia and reverses for the ally Bulgaria, the balance of power there had been altered without Austrian guidance, Rumania was now moving increasingly into the Russian camp and there was the prospect of a new Balkan League which, having already dealt with one decaying imperial power in the area, would now turn to the next. The advice constantly pressed from the army Chief of Staff was becoming increasingly difficult to resist. In January 1913, Conrad had, without waiting for a pretext, proposed war against Serbia. In October he had strongly supported the threat of strong action which had made the Serbians ready to retreat from the advanced positions they occupied in Albania, but neither power had regarded that as a final settlement. Early in 1914 Berchtold blamed Germany for the Dual Monarchy's loss of prestige and announced his set intention of dealing aggressively with the threat on the next opportunity. By June he had in draft a letter to Berlin pressing for its assistance in first, forcing Rumania to choose the side she would adhere to and second, in binding Bulgaria to the Triple Alliance. Germany must join with Austria-Hungary in resisting the steady deterioration in the position of the two powers. The army for its part was doing something to reassert Austrian prestige in the Balkans: there were to be manoeuvres in northern Bosnia in June, the display of Austrian power would influence an area showing too great a fondness for Serbia and, to add to the impact, the Inspector General of the Forces, Archduke Franz Ferdinand, heir to the throne, would attend.

The difficulties of civil authorities in the face of growing military power was obvious in many European countries and Serbia was no exception. Păsić, the premier, was confronted by Colonel Apis, the head of the Serbian military intelligence and principal figure in a secret society which ran an anti-government newspaper. The society, which came to be termed the Black Hand, had the impedimenta of a comic-opera conspiracy including a seal composed of a skull and crossbones flag, a knife, a pistol and poison, but it was seriously dedicated to political terrorism. One strand in political radicalism in the past (and down to today) has been those who sought to secure change by selective political assassination. Members of this organisation included those who had assassinated the last Serbian king and thus established the new dynasty. There were also those who had engaged in resistance movements in Macedonia when it had been under Turkish rule and in Bosnia under Austrian rule. This society had therefore weapons, experience and contacts and it was natural that those contemplating a political assassination should approach it.

THE ASSASSINATION AT SARAJEVO

The initiative for the assassination of Archduke Franz Ferdinand seems to have come from some students who belonged to a broad movement known as Young Bosnia, a pro-Slav organisation dedicated to the overthrow of imperial rule and the establishment of democracy. Gavrilo Princip, a nineteen year old student, resolved with some colleagues to secure weapons and assassinate Franz Ferdinand, believing in the words of a Serbian poem he admired 'Even if we have not created anything ourselves we shall at least have put an end to the misery of our time.' Arms and facilities for travelling across the border were supplied by the Black Hand, if not officially, at least through some of its members. Pasic received a report of the movement of the assassins if not their intentions, which can, however, scarcely have been obscure. After an unsuccessful bomb attempt by one of the conspirators, Princip shot the Archduke and his wife on 28 June 1914.

It was, of course, an inconvenient time of the year for an international crisis; statesmen and service chiefs were away on summer holidays. Still it is striking how little was the impact of assassination. The report of the British Consul at Sarajevo was chiefly concerned with insurance on consular property damaged by the bomb blast. In Paris, the Socialist newspaper *L'Humanité* described it as 'one more rivulet in the stream of blood that has flown in vain on the Balkan peninsula', although some other French newspapers raised the possibility that the Austrian government might use the excuse to take strong measures against Serbia. That was the nub of the issue; if the Austrian government decided to redress its grievance by direct action against Serbia then there was chance of a major war. The Austrian army, predictably, pressed for action; the Bosnian military governor, Potiorek claimed that forcible intervention in Serbia was the only response and Conrad called for mobilisation. Berchtold fenced a little, being afraid of the possibility of a revolution within the empire if war were declared, and prepared a diplomatic case by looking for evidence of Serbian complicity in the assassination. The initial results

Pǎsić, Prime Minister of Serbia

Sazanov, Russian Foreign Minister

Bethmann-Hollweg,
German Foreign Minister

Jaurès, French Socialist leader

Delcassé, French Foreign Minister

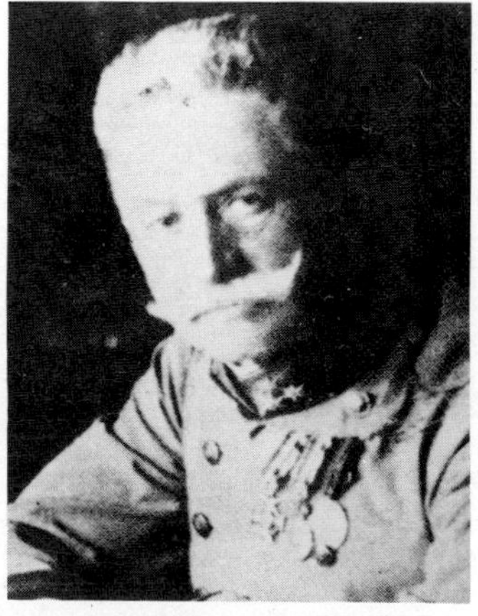

Conrad von Hötzendorf,
Austrian Commander-in-Chief

Fig. 6 - *Pre-war Office-holders.*

Fig. 7 – *Diplomacy Exhausted.* Prince Lichnowsky, the German Ambassador in London, crosses the Horse Guards Parade near the Foreign Office on the day of the British declaration of war.

seemed to strengthen this view, but there could be no question of Austria-Hungary taking military action against Serbia without German support in case Austrian forces would be left with their flank exposed. Thus it was that the letter drafted before the assassination calling for German support in a new and vigorous Balkan policy was given a final paragraph to cover the latest development and sent to Berlin.

The German reaction only makes sense when seen against the background of what was regarded as Berchtold's vacillating policy. There had been talk of strong measures in the past and then procrastination and withdrawal, which had been blamed on German counsels of caution. Although the language was stronger on this occasion, there was no certainty that the Austrian government was entirely serious. Still, the Kaiser gave no reason for delay on the German side, urging that the time was opportune for a war against Serbia and, even if Russia intervened, German support would be assured. This was the notorious 'blank cheque' of 6 July. Not only did this promise go beyond the terms of the Dual Alliance which had not provided for German support if Austria provoked Russia, but it made more precise the assurances the Kaiser had given in the past. Support was also promised for the attempt to bring Bulgaria into the Triple Alliance.

In Rome there was little enthusiasm for supporting the Austrian case. The Dual Monarchy had three quarters of a million Italian subjects and they were in a majority in some areas, Trieste for example. The friction caused by the Italian desire for the recovery of these 'unredeemed' subjects was compounded by the differences between the two allies over the Adriatic coast of the Balkans. Indeed, in early 1914 the Italians contributed to the Austrian frustration by thwarting a plan for the incorporation of Montenegro in Albania, the better to keep Serbia from the sea. Against this background, Italian unreliability as a member of the Triple Alliance is understandable: they quickly made plain their refusal to take part in a war which was not caused by aggression against their allies. To do so would have been to exceed the provisions of the alliance. They consistently adopted this view and hence declared their neutrality in August.

THE AUSTRIAN REACTION

A Council of Ministers met in Vienna on 7 July in which Berchtold sided with the army in agreeing that diplomatic successes were not enough; Serbia would have to be humiliated by force of arms thus strengthening the Empire internally, especially in Bosnia, and convincing Rumania of the futility of joining a new Balkan League. Tisza, the Hungarian Premier emerges, however, as the dominant figure in these discussions. Having no wish to see the Empire gain more Slavs and thus weaken the Magyar position, he secured agreement that there were to be no annexations of Serbian territory. He successfully resisted two ideas strongly supported by the army, immediate mobilisation and an invasion without prior declaration of war. Using his effective veto because of his control over the use of Hungarian troops, he managed single-handed to prevent a final decision for war being taken. An ultimatum was to be prepared with his assent and it would leave open the possibility of a diplomatic victory if Serbia accepted but war if the Serbian government made any reservations. Emperor Francis Joseph, like Tisza, did not at first rule out a diplomatic solution but both men gradually came around to Berchtold's view that the demands made on Serbia must be so severe as to make rejection virtually certain. Despite the apparent calm in Berlin with the major figures on holiday, continued encouragement was given to the Austro-Hungarian government to act promptly. The reasons for the German government's attitude have, in the last decade, been re-examined in the light of its aims during the war. Fritz Fischer and others have amply documented the German desire for expansion, the succession of plans from September 1914 onwards for the creation of an extensive central European empire as well as a large body of territory in Africa. That suggested the need for a fresh look at the pre-war German attitudes and from that has come a picture of Bethmann, the German Chancellor, as the voice of these expansionist interests rather than the moderate statesman of traditional German history. Moreover, the interests he embodied, says Fischer, were not the preserve of rabid nationalists such as the Pan-German League but represented the consensus of German opinion. In short, Germany launched war in 1914 in pursuit of its imperialist ambitions. The chief critic of this view, the late Gerhard Ritter, played down the importance of the war aims as being unrepresentative views formulated in exceptional circumstances. He stressed the moderation of the politicians and emphasised instead the important role of the High Command caught with its inflexible Schlieffen plan.

Still, the German support for Austria in July 1914 was decisive, and even Ritter admits that it was the political authorities in Berlin rather than the professional soldiers in Vienna who pressed for war. All circumstances pointed to the advantages of the summer of 1914 for Austria to pursue this policy: the British, tied up with the Irish problem, could be expected to remain neutral, the French not only had their own domestic problems but the change-over to a three-year recruitment period had left the army temporarily in confusion. Both these nations might thus be expected to restrain Russia. The German government, well informed on Russian affairs, knew that this was an inconvenient time for war for Russia whereas, by about 1917, the military changes and increases would have put the Central

Powers very much at a disadvantage. Even at that moment the Russian forces in Galicia were under strength while the men were absent gathering the harvest. Moreover, it was rare to have so good an issue on which to launch a war, for the murder was widely denounced even in the democracies. Some delay was however inescapable while investigations of the assassinations continued, and the harvest in Austria-Hungary was collected.

It would also be best if the crisis came after the French President Poincaré had completed his visit to St Petersburg. Thus the date for delivery of the note making the demands on Serbia was finally fixed for 23 July. Although the German government saw the note only in its final form shortly before its presentation, the main provisions were made known to it over the fortnight of drafting. As early as 18 July a Bavarian diplomat had been able to report, after discussions at the Foreign Ministry in Berlin, the substance of the proposed ultimatum. 'It is perfectly plain', he wrote, 'that Serbia cannot accept any such demands which are incompatible with her dignity as a sovereign state. Thus the result will be war. Here they are absolutely willing that Austria should take advantage of this favourable opportunity, even at the risk of further complications'. There was to be a 48-hour deadline for unconditional acceptance, the Serbian government was to publish a declaration condemning the propaganda against Austria-Hungary, it was to accept the help of Austrian officials in suppressing in Serbia movements against Austria-Hungary, to institute an enquiry, again with Austrian participation, and to arrest certain Serbian officials apparently implicated in the assassination.

Without over-simplifying too much, the developments since the end of June might be summarised as follows. The Austro-Hungarian government had found itself faced with a deteriorating position in the Balkans and resolved, in so far as its curiously indecisive and divided structure would allow, to take firm action possibly involving war with Serbia. The Sarajevo assassination provided the occasion for such action. In this decision it was given unequivocal support by the German government, which indeed urged it along the way. The German government was concerned that delay would lessen the chance of a localised Austro-Serbian war and feared that the elements of doubt temporarily dissipated in the Dual Monarchy would quickly return. It was also influenced by the seemingly suitable conjunction of circumstances for a preventive war before the military improvements of other nations took full effect. More important was the belief expressed by Jagow, the German Foreign Secretary, 'The maintenance of Austria, and, in fact, of the most powerful Austria possible, is a necessity for us for both internal and external reasons.' The continuity of German policy at the Foreign ministry is striking, for Holstein had long stressed the same needs of maintaining the Prussian position in Germany by keeping the Dual Monarchy strong and bolstering the Dual Alliance, which was as strong as its weaker partner.

The delivery of the Austrian ultimatum changed the character of the crisis. Until its terms were announced, it seemed not unreasonable to expect localisation; a negotiated settlement could be reached by the Serbians conceding the more reasonable demands of the Austrians. Such had been the pattern in the past; an action was taken by one power and an answering demand made by another. The conflict did not escalate because the allies of the powers concerned restrained them, while showing readiness to resist any extreme demands. The claims made always had an escape clause, some road to compromise was left open so that both powers could retreat from conflict with honour intact, although status might be increased or lessened. This was a different case. For most of those concerned in making policy in Vienna and Berlin a Serbian acceptance of the demands was neither expected nor desired. The possibility of compromise was lessened by the forty-eight hour limit imposed on the time for reply and the refusal of Vienna, although under pressure from the powers, to accept any prolongation. 'What you want is war,' Sazanov told the Austrian Ambassador in St Petersburg on reading the ultimatum, 'and you have burned your bridges behind you.' Grey thought the ultimatum the most formidable document presented by one independent power to another, perhaps failing to appreciate the 'colonial' status Serbia had in the eyes of the Central Powers. Partly for this reason, the German government refused to co-operate in proposals for a compromise put forward by the Russian and British governments. The German argument was always that this was an Austrian problem and other powers should not intervene. We might say in retrospect that the localising of the war, the exclusion of other powers from a mediatory role, was unreal. The German government continued to work towards that possibility of a limited Austro-Serbian war while, of course, still preparing for the risk of wider conflict. They based this on the belief that, firstly, Russia did not want war at this time and, secondly, swift action with firm German backing combined with the Austrian readiness not to annex any significant part of Serbia, (a piece of self-denial based on the Hungarian reluctance to have more Slavs in the empire) would present the powers with a *fait accompli.*

THE RUSSIAN ATTITUDE AND THE SERBIAN ANSWER

The first German assumption was not without some substance for Russia was, on any objective assessment, unready for war – in two or three years time, yes, but not at a time of serious internal unrest, inept military leadership and inadequate equipment and training. Police suppression exacerbated the situation; the Austrian representative in Russia reported to Berchtold on 17 July 1914, 'If one continues ... [to keep] all safety valves closed, it can happen that the revolutionary organisation of Russia will be completed before her military one.' On the other hand, Sazonov believed that the people would rally behind the government in the event of war. Moreover, the possibility of an Austro-Serb conflict had been foreseen as early as January and Russian support would include, it was agreed, intervention on the Serbian side. This consistent line in Russian policy was reinforced by the visit of the French President, Poincaré and the Premier, Viviani, to Russia immediately before the delivery of the ultimatum. The French assurances of support were apparently very encouraging and were made to sound even more so in the following weeks by the bellicose French Ambassador, Paléologue.

Against this background, the Russian Council of Ministers decided on 24 July to encourage the Great Powers to intervene to prevent war. Serbia was much weakened by the strain of the Balkan wars and the Russian advice was not to resist any Austrian attack but rather to fall back and appeal for assistance from the Great Powers. Such an action would tend to make the Austrian ultimatum seem even more unreasonable. A further step in this direction was the Serbian reply to the ultimatum. Presumably Russian advice contributed to the character of that reply, although we cannot be sure for the Serbian government documents are only now being prepared for publication. This was a soft answer calculated, not so much to turn away wrath, which they regarded as inevitable, but to put Austria in the wrong. Almost all the demands were met and the Kaiser was substantially correct to describe it later as 'a capitulation of the most humiliating kind'. Still on certain points, for example, the participation by Austrian officials in an enquiry into the plot, reservations were made and the readiness to put all the proposals into operation might have been doubted. The Austrian government immediately broke off diplomatic relations. Serbian mobilisation started even before the reply was presented and Austrian partial mobilisation began the same day.

MOBILISATION

Mobilisation posed a new problem in crisis management for European statesmen and, apart from the Balkan wars, there was little past experience on which to draw. The diplomatic steps leading from a state of peace, or at least non-war, to war were familiar, but it was not clear where mobilisation belonged in the sequence. To make matters worse, the operation had several phases and the diplomatic significance of each was unclear, especially since it was difficult for countries to keep in step because the speed of mobilisation differed. No nation wished to be caught unprepared, but none wished to provoke retaliatory action by the others. If a nation wished to declare the 'Period Preparatory to War' which involved, for example, bringing the complement of men in fortresses up to strength or if it wished to declare a mobilisation of some areas but not of others it was essential to know exactly what was involved, how it affected further steps in mobilisation if they became necessary and how other nations were likely to react. That presumed the subordination of the military to the political wings of government and close liaison between the two. Pre-war militarism rendered that unlikely in most countries. At the Russian Council of Ministers that considered the Austrian ultimatum to Serbia, it had been decided to draw up the decrees for partial mobilisation and hold them in readiness. On the following day, 26 July, the period preparatory to war was declared and throughout Russia military preparations started. These measures were encouraged by the French military leaders who were themselves recalling troops away for the harvest or in Morocco. Joffre and others were chiefly concerned that Russia should direct its forces against Germany, for without that diversion in the east, France would have to bear all the weight of the German invasion when war came. An early start to Russian mobilisation seemed all the more necessary because the projected Russian strategic railways had not been completed.

BRITISH HESITATION

As early as 24 July the British Ambassador in St Petersburg had reported that the French and Russians were determined to make a strong stand against the Austrian ultimatum. At the British Foreign Office one official wrote: 'Our interests are tied up with those of France and Russia in this struggle, which is not for the possession of Serbia, but one between Germany aiming at a political dictatorship in Europe and the Powers who desire to retain individual liberty.' Grey did not see it in this light. He continued to hold the belief that the conflict might be contained and refused to commit the British government while the dispute was Austro-Serbian. He had little choice, for to fight for Serbia was not a rallying call either in the Cabinet or the country at large. The most that could be agreed was a measure to keep the fleet concentrated near Portland on the Dorset coast rather than dispersing to its various routine tasks. Grey cast about for some way of averting the coming crisis, proposing joint intervention by the powers and later a conference such as had been instrumental in resolving the previous Balkan dispute. But on the Tuesday (28 July) Asquith, the Prime Minister noted in his diary the failure of the proposal and assumed that 'nothing but a miracle' could avert a war, although it was by no means clear that Britain would participate. On the previous day, Asquith had been almost entirely taken up with the Irish question, for the conference to bring peace there had broken down a few days before and, with gun-running incidents, all seemed set for civil war. Thus neither the political nor the public mind was ready for decisive action. The French government was leaderless with Poincaré and Viviani still not back in Paris and the British Ambassador reported his opinion that France would not support Russia in a Balkan war. Grey tried to get the Cabinet to decide that it would fight alongside France if war with the Central Powers started, but it split. To have forced the issue would have divided both the Cabinet and the Liberal party and would have sent Asquith, Grey and some followers into war in alliance with the Conservatives. This very unwelcome prospect acted as a further brake on British action in these days.

THE AUSTRO-SERBIAN WAR 28 JULY

The German government had watched the Russian steps towards mobilisation without distress. Such moves tended to put Russia in the position of the aggressor thus giving a moral advantage to the Triple Alliance and promising well for war in favourable circumstances. Within Germany it would reduce the probability of Social Democrat opposition to the war while at the same reinforcing working-class opposition to the war in the Entente countries. More embarrassing diplomatically were the constant requests to Berlin to join in attempts at mediation. The German government had denied all knowledge of the terms of the Austrian ultimatum until just before its submission, although their denial was little believed, for many European diplomats recognised that Austria would not have moved without consulting and securing the support of its partner. To keep up the pretence, however, the German government had to pass on to Vienna proposals for mediation, while secretly denying support to them. Conrad would have gladly postponed the declaration of war until mobilisation was complete on 12 August. However, in answer to pressure from the diplomats both in Vienna and Berlin who were anxious to cut short these mediatory attempts, war was declared on 28 July. The bombardment of Belgrade across the Danube started shortly afterwards.

The work of the diplomats did not end with the outbreak of war between Austria and Serbia, indeed the flow of documents increased to a flood. The week which saw a Balkan war become a world war put tremendous strain on policy-makers throughout Europe; Cabinet meetings at 2 a.m., negotiation in dressing gowns and mounting exhaustion all round. It was a classic recipe for crisis mismanagement as the increasingly pressing demands of the military shortened the timetable. Negotiations for containment of the war and preparations for its escalation were two sides of one coin, although we can separate them for exposition.

Grey's desire for peace was sincere. His words, 'I hate war, I hate war,' came from the heart. Still as late as 1 August the bulk of the Liberal party favoured a declaration that Britain would in no circumstances take a hand, so he was unable to make fully clear to either side where Britain would stand in the event of war, a position that put heavy strains on the Entente and allowed the German government to continue to believe in the possibility of British neutrality. On 29 July, Grey made it plain to the German Ambassador that neutrality could not be relied upon while affirming to the French that British help could not be assumed in a conflict arising from the French alliance with Russia. He advanced a succession of compromise proposals, but they tripped up on the idea of a conference, for there were memories in Vienna of her reverses at the 1913 London Ambassadors' conference. Alternatively, they involved an end to mobilisation, which was unacceptable in Russia, or obliged the Austrian army and people to satisfy themselves with less than the victory over Serbia they anticipated. Even after the Russian and German armies had mobilised, the German Ambassador cabled a proposal from London that if France were not invaded, Britain and France would remain neutral. Although it proved a misunderstanding, the Kaiser, interestingly enough, called a halt to the mobilisation in the west and sent for champagne. He would well have had cause for celebration for the prime object of the German policy in these days had been securing British neutrality.

If the British peace moves were partly the product of domestic politics, German negotiations were directed at securing the best possible framework for the coming war. The most obvious, and inept, attempt to keep Britain neutral came on 30 July when, in exchange for British neutrality, Bethmann promised, in the event of a successful war, not to take territory from France, Belgium and Holland. For the German government it was also desirable that Russia be put in the wrong. Admiral von Müller, of the Kaiser's circle, reflected 'The government has succeeded very well in making us appear as the attacked.' The personal telegrams exchanged between the Kaiser and the Tsar were applauded by Bethmann as contributing to this end. At the same time it would be wrong to discount the desire of 'Willy' and 'Nicky' (as they addressed each other) to avoid war and such intervention did influence the Tsar to alter the decree for general mobilisation of 29 July to one of partial mobilisation. Still, the diplomatic preparation and the announcement of Russian general mobilisation on 30 July (before the German mobilisation) quietened Socialist doubts and assured German national unity for war. Nor was there any weakening at Vienna. Cabinet met there on the morning of 31 July to consider the British proposal for mediation based on the Austrian occupation of Belgrade and other places prior to negotiation. The German government had seemingly supported the proposal but in fact emphasised the need to give an impression of seriously considering it. No minister had a word to say in its favour. Even Tisza, the Hungarian Prime Minister, had no thought of stopping the war and suggested that the government name continuance of military operation and stopping of Russian mobilisation as two preliminary conditions to considering it. The Finance Minister thought that an extremely clever way of gaining time while making a soothing reply.

The diplomatic search for peace – or preparation for war – was, over this last week, outstripped by the demands of the service chiefs and the technical constraints of the mobilisation schemes. The Kaiser, seeing Britain rallying to France, remarked that Edward VII dead was more influential than he was alive and it might be said that Schlieffen dead was more influential than many of the living statesmen and soldiers who tried to escape his iron timetable. Mobilisation plans, or the lack of them, posed many problems. In Russia partial mobilisation of the southern military districts had begun on 25 July but there were no complete plans for it. It contravened the military arrangements with France and endangered the possibility of effective general mobilisation, because that would involve countermanding many of the orders sent out and would lead to chaos on the railways and elsewhere. The Austro-Hungarian partial mobilisation had started and was directed towards Serbia. There was provision in Conrad's complex mobilisation scheme for reversing the movement, up to the fifth day of mobilisation, of some of the troops back to Galicia to face a Russian threat. Despite German pressure, mobilisation against Russia was delayed until 31 July and the declaration of war and the beginning of the reversal of the troop movements was not made until 6 August. That was significant for several reasons. Firstly, the Russo-German war began five days before the Russo-Austrian war, its presumed cause. Secondly, the change in direction of mobilisation was too late to be incorporated in the system, confused it, and resulted in the troops leaving Serbia too early to secure victory and arriving in Galicia too late to prevent defeat. Thirdly, it broke the arrangement made with the German High Command whereby the Russian threat would be met by a strong Austrian force aided by a smaller German attack across the Narva. As Norman Stone remarks, the episode provides 'striking evidence that Austria-Hungary was resolved to solve her South Slav difficulties first through, and then despite, a European war.'

In Berlin, a major conflict between the civil and the military leadership was shaping. Moltke could see little chance of the Italians and Rumanians marching alongside the Germans. The Austro-Hungarian army seemed preoccupied with Serbia, although fifty-five divisions of Russian troops were being mobilised. Moreover, on 31 July other news was coming through of the extent of the Russian military preparations. The Schlieffen plan worked on a six week period for Russian mobilisation during which time the conquest of France should be so complete as to allow the return of German forces to the east. The Russian mobilisation, which had started in a limited way on 26 July, put the plan in jeopardy and it became urgent to clarify the situation by mobilising German forces. In the west, another element of the timetable troubled him. If the great sweep through Belgium was to be successful, Liège must be taken by the third day of mobilisation, yet Belgium was neutral, so it must be presented with an ultimatum. These crucial considerations were coloured, however, by his knowing that a prior Russian mobilisation would strengthen the government's case at the outbreak of war. The eminent German scholar Gerhard Ritter stresses Moltke's restraint while others emphasise his desire for early mobilisation but there is agreement that on 30 July news of the progress of the Russian mobilisation lead him to telegraph Conrad: 'Mobilise at once against Russia. Germany will mobilise.' He also made renewed attempts to convert Bethmann to this viewpoint and secured a promise of a decision by midday on 31 July.

In St Petersburg the Tsar was under heavy pressure to order general mobilisation. The generals were aware that the continued partial mobilisation would hamper the general mobilisation which was, argued Sazanov, essential because it was plain that Germany desired war since she refused all attempts at a peaceful settlement. The French Ambassador, contrary to his Prime Minister who was just then cabling restraint, urged general mobilisation on the grounds that the French government might be talked into remaining neutral, unless Russia adhered to the Dual Alliance by a full mobilisation. The Tsar reluctantly ordered general mobilisation, news of which arrived in Berlin at five minutes before the twelve o'clock deadline. The mastery of the military over the civil rulers, obvious with the tone of Moltke's correspondence with Conrad, now became more obvious. A twelve-hour ultimatum to France demanding to know whether it would remain neutral was despatched. This was required by the Schlieffen plan for operations against France had to start quickly, but the French refused to declare themselves. The military grew impatient with diplomatic preparations and pressed for an undeclared invasion of France.

The centre of interest now moved to Belgium, although this was not immediately obvious. Neutral Belgium, until the outbreak of the Austro-Serbian war, had its defences directed against Britain and France as well as Germany. It was sceptical of Britain, the chief guarantor of its neutrality under the treaty of 1839. The neutrality of Belgium acquired a great importance in Britain for it was one of the few points on which the disjointed Cabinet could agree. They could not agree to fight for Serbia which was small and distant, nor for Russia which was autocratic and unpopular. They refused to see any general undertaking to France derived from secret talks authorised by a few ministers or an exchange of notes by which the two governments promised to consult in the event of war. They would however agree on certain compromise measures that plainly involved British interests: the defence of the north French coast and the channel which was important for shipping and the guarantee of Belgium, a legal obligation and a strategic precaution if the channel was to be kept free for British shipping. To prepare the ground, Grey asked for promises from both the French and German governments that they would respect Belgian neutrality. The French made such a promise; the Germans could not, for the Schlieffen plan precluded it. The German declaration of war on Russia was made on 1 August. While the French government started mobilisation on the same day, they did not fulfil their alliance obligations to Russia by declaring war on Germany. Failing that excuse for war, the German government claimed certain border violations by the French as a justification for the declaration of war on 3 August. The Belgian government having refused a German request for the free passage of troops, the German army entered Belgium on 4 August to take the great fortress of Liége and Britain declared war the same day. Many Germans, from Bethmann down, found it difficult to think that Britain would forsake its own neutrality for Belgium's. The Belgian issue, secondary though it was, was a sufficient moral fixing-point. The mistake was to believe in the possibility of continued British neutrality in the face of German expansion. The First World War was, in that sense, Fritz Fischer's 'War of Illusion'.

CONCLUSION

Contemporaries did not expect the war in the summer of 1914 and, once started, did not expect it to last long. There was, however, an awareness of the prospect of war throughout these years. Germany's industrial leadership was clearly perceived and the contrast with her international political role noted. Russia, the United States and Britain seemed destined to be world powers in the twentieth century. Would Germany be the fourth? The views of General Bernhardi usually only represented that influential pressure group, the Pan-German League. He was, however, expressing a widely held view when he wrote, in 1912,

> Today there can be no question of a *European* states system but only of a *world states system,* in which the balance of power rests on real power factors. In this states system one must strive to gain, at the head of a central European confederation, a position of equal rights, by in one way or another reducing the alleged European balance of power to its true value and correspondingly increasing our own power.

In pursuit of this world policy the German government built a navy strong enough to threaten the Royal Navy but not strong enough to conquer it, in foreign relations they challenged everybody, as Bethmann admitted, but weakened nobody. In the name of the 'balance of power' other nations strengthened their armies, their navies and their alliances, thus raising the German fear of encirclement. That was heightened still further by the obvious weakness of Austria-Hungary. An informed observer perceived two policies in conflict within Germany. *Weltpolitik* was, in his view, now discounted and the replacement was to be either defensive concentration in central Europe or a preventive war to extinguish the dreaded Franco-Russian threat. Writing in June 1914 he claimed that the former would prevail but the following month proved him wrong. (R.C. Long, 'The End of Weltpolitik', *Fortnightly Review,* June 1914, p.992). Talk of the supersession of *Weltpolitik* was perhaps a little misleading. It remained important, although officials, in order to prepare the public mind for war, chose to emphasise the threat from abroad. Indeed, the main achievement of the Fischer school of historians has been to stress the importance of the German desire for economic and territorial expansion. Historical revisions have a way, however, of sometimes pushing old truths into the shadows. That the war arose from a Balkan conflict was not accidental. The long history that was behind the Austrian decision to resolve its Balkan difficulties by war must retain its central position.

The expansionist ambitions of the Entente powers were obviously more limited than those of the Central Powers. Still, those nations contributed to the start of the war by their diplomatic and military preparations for it. Contemporaries sometimes justified these steps in terms of the maintenance of the so-called 'balance of power'. N.H. Brailsford, an English radical writing just before the war, termed it 'a metaphor of venerable hypocrisy which only serves to disguise the perennial struggle for power and predominance'. Changes of status within the European system would occur; if they were to be contained there would need to be provisions for collective security and peaceful change. War was, however, necessary to drive the lesson home and create a League of Nations. The pre-war alliance system prevented free international negotiations and hamstrung even such small attempts at concerted European action as the London Ambassadors' conference.

Part of the inheritance from the war-guilt controversy has been the temptation to apportion blame nation by nation, a procedure that might obscure those causes of war that were shared by all or most of the powers. Contemporaries were, for example, in no doubt about the dominance of militarism in Europe although the meaning they attached to the word was sometimes imprecise. German society was influenced by military values and an assumption of the moral worth of war. Nor were other countries free of the same attitude. Even in Britain, where there were strong traditions of opposition to military display or influence, there was evidence of the growth of military sentiment. That in turn derived strength from the fierce loyalties aroused by nation and empire. The power of these sincerely held beliefs is understandable, but they still served other purposes. They were fostered as a suitable dressing for many class, group or party interests within the European nations. 'Surely it is not without significance', writes Arno Mayer, 'that nearly all the superpatriots who clamoured for preparedness and foreign policy pugnacity held reactionary, ultra-conservative or proto-fascist views on domestic affairs.'

APPENDICES

CHRONOLOGICAL TABLES

A. Major Diplomatic Events 1894-1914

1894	4	Jan	Franco-Russian alliance
1902	30	Jan	Anglo-Japanese alliance
1904	8	April	*Entente Cordiale*
1905	1	April	Kaiser's landing at Tangier (First Moroccan Crisis)
1906	1	Jan	Start of Anglo-French military conversations
1906	16	Jan	Opening of Algeciras Conference
1907	31	Aug	Anglo-Russian agreement
1908	6	Oct	Dual Monarchy annexes Bosnia-Herzegovina
1909	24	Feb	British Cabinet resolves naval scare with proposal for eight dreadnoughts 1909-10
1909	31	March	Serbia accepts Austrian annexation of Bosnia
1911	1	July	*Panther* at Agadir (Second Moroccan Crisis)
1911	21	July	Lloyd George's Mansion House speech
1912		Jan	German elections – Socialists the strongest party
1912	7	Feb	Haldane mission to Berlin
1912	17	Oct	Outbreak of first Balkan war
1913		June	Reichstag passes bill to enlarge army
1913	30	June	Outbreak of second Balkan war
1913	7	Aug	French Army Bill imposing three year military service service
1913	10	Aug	Treaty of Bucharest
1913	20	Nov	Zabern incident
1914	28	June	Assassination of Archduke Franz Ferdinand

B. The Crisis of July-August 1914

July	**6**	The 'Blank Cheque' assuring the Austro-Hungarian Emperor that Germany would stand behind him in his dealings with Serbia
	20	Poincaré starts visit to Russia
	23	Austro-Hungarian ultimatum to Serbia
	25	Serbian reply to the ultimatum
	28	Austro-Hungarian declaration of war on Serbia
	29	Grey warns Germany not to count on British neutrality and France not to count on British intervention
	30	French troops sent to within ten kilometres of the frontier Russian decision for general mobilisation Moltke calls on Conrad to mobilise against Russia

	31	German mobilisation decided and ultimatums to Russia (demanding a stop to mobilisation) and France (to declare her neutrality) British enquiries of Germany and France: would they respect Belgian neutrality?
August	1	German declaration of war on Russia French order of general mobilisation
	2	German advance into Luxemburg and request for passage through Belgium
	3	Belgium rejects German request Italy declares neutrality Germany declares war on France
	4	German troops cross into Belgium Britain and Germany at war
	6	Austria-Hungary declares war on Russia

SOME PROMINENT OFFICE-HOLDERS

Aehrenthal, Count von (1854-1912) Austro-Hungarian Foreign Secretary 1906-12

Asquith, Herbert (1858-1928) British Liberal Prime Minister 1908-16

Berchtold, Count Leopold von (1863-1942) Austro-Hungarian Foreign Minister 1912-15

Bethmann-Hollweg, Theobald von (1856-1921) German Chancellor 1909-17

Campbell-Bannerman, Sir Henry (1836-1908) British Liberal Prime Minister 1905-08

Churchill, Winston S. (1874-1965) First Lord of the Admiralty 1911-15

Conrad von Hötzendorf, Count Franz (1852-1925) Austro-Hungarian Chief of General Staff 1906-11, 1912-17

Delcassé, Théophile (1852-1923) French Foreign Minister 1898-1905

Fisher, John, 1st Baron (1841-1920) First Sea Lord 1904-10, 1914-15

Grey, Sir Edward (1862-1933) British Foreign Secretary 1905-16

Haldane, Richard B. (1856-1928) British Secretary of State for War 1905-1912, Lord Chancellor 1912-15

Izvolsky, Aleksandr (1856-1919) Russian Foreign Minister 1906-10 Ambassador to France 1910-17

Jagow, Gottlieb von (1863-1938) German State Secretary for Foreign Affairs 1913-16

Jaurès, Jean (1859-1914) Leader of the French Socialist Party (Section francaise de l'internationale ouvrière) 1906-14

Joffre, Joseph (1852-1931) Commander-in-Chief of the French armies in 1914

Lloyd George, David (1863-1945) British Chancellor of the Exchequer 1908-15

Moltke, Count Helmuth von (1848-1916) German Chief of the General Staff 1906-14

Pašić, Nikola (?1845-1928) Serbian Prime Minister and Minister of Foreign Affairs 1908-18

Poincaré, Raymond (1860-1934) French Premier 1911-13, President 1913-20

Sazanov, Sergei (1866-1927) Russian Minister of Foreign Affairs 1910-16

Tirpitz, Alfred von (1849-1930) State Secretary of the German Navy 1898-1916

Viviani, René (1862-195) French Premier and Minister of Foreign Affairs 1914-15

READING GUIDE

There is no satisfactory synthesis in English of the latest research on the causes of the First World War. It is impossible to list all the recent articles where the revisions in our view of the war still lie buried, although some of them are given more permanent form in H.W. Koch, *The Origins of the First World War* (Macmillan pbk 1972). The most important scholarly journals on this subject are *The Journal of Contemporary History* (especially 1966), *Past and Present* (1966), *The Journal of Modern History* and *The Historical Journal.*

Since the causes of the war have to be seen in the context of the European history of the period, it would perhaps be wisest to start with a general history, such as J.K. Munholland, *Origins of Contemporary Europe 1890-1914* (Harcourt Brace paperback). A satisfactory introduction is provided by J. Remak, *The Origins of World War I* (Holt, Rinehart & Winston 1967) or L.D. Lafore, *The Long Fuse* (Lippincott 1965) but both have to be supplemented at a number of points. Particularly good on the impact of pre-war military planning are: A.J.P. Taylor, *War by Time-Table* (Macdonald 1969) which has a great many illustrations but is concentrated on the immediate prelude to the war and L.C.F. Turner, *Origins of the First World War* (Edward Arnold 1970), a short work that incorporates his important studies of the mobilisation schemes.

Modern German history is going through a period of radical revision. The early work of Professor F. Fischer and his associates was focussed on the aims of Germany during the war and demonstrated to the satisfaction of many, but not all, of their colleagues the important of German imperialism in those years. This debate is dealt with in J.A. Moses, *The War Aims of Imperial Germany* (University of Queensland Press 1968) and Gerald Feldman, *German Imperialism 1914-18: the Development of an Historical Debate* (Wiley pb. 1972). The same attention was not given to the pre-war years although the general way in which the Fischer school sees those years is sketched in the early part of I. Geiss, *July 1914, the Outbreak of the First World War* (Batsford 1967) which includes a very interesting collection of documents. Fischer has now turned his attention to the earlier period with *Kreig der Illusionen* (1969). There is a valuable long review of this work in *Revue Historique* no. 497, Jan. 1971, P. Renouvin 'Nationalisme et Imperialisme en Allemagne de 1911 à 1914'. On imperialism more widely, there is H. Gollwitzer *Europe in the Age of Imperialism 1880-1914* (Thames and Hudson 1969), and M.M. and M.R. Stenson *Imperialism 1870-1914* (a Heinemann Monograph 1972).

If we are to look beyond the frontiers of traditional studies of the war origins, these two thought provoking essays must be read: J. Joll, *1914 The Unspoken Assumptions* (London School of Economics, 1968) and A. Mayer, 'Domestic Causes of the First World War' in L. Krieger and F. Stern, *The Responsibility of Power, Historical Essays in Honor of Hajo Holborn* (Macmillan 1967).

Finally, some reading on special aspects of the period:

G. Haupt, *Socialism and the Great War* (Clarendon Press, Oxford 1972)

M. Kitchen, *The German Officer Corps 1890-1914* (Clarendon Press, Oxford 1968)

G. Ritter, *The Problem of Militarism in Germany* (Allen Lane, 1972) – to be used with some caution

K. Robbins, *Sir Edward Grey* (Cassell 1971)

J. Steinberg, *Tirpitz and the Birth of the German Battle Fleet; Yesterday's Deterrent* (Macdonald, 1968)

E.L. Woodward, *Great Britain and the German Navy* (Clarendon Press, Oxford 1935)

F.R. Bridge, *From Sadowa to Sarajevo* (Austrian Foreign Policy) (Routledge & Kegan Paul 1972).